Shakespeare
MADE EASY

Henry V

WITHDRAWN

*Modern English version
side-by-side with full original text*

Modernised by Alan Durband

Nelson Thornes

Originally published 1989 by Hutchinson Education

Reprinted 1990 by
Stanley Thornes (Publishers) Ltd
Delta Place
27 Bath Road
CHELTENHAM
GL53 7TH
United Kingdom

Reprinted Under New ISBN in 1999

12 13 / 10 9 8 7 6 5 4 3

A catalogue record for this book is available from the British
Library.

ISBN 978 0 7487 4373 5

Photoset in Plantin and Univers

Printed by Multivista Global Ltd

'Reade him, therefore, and againe, and againe: And if then you do not like him, surely you are in some danger, not to understand him . . .'

John Hemming
Henry Condell

Preface to the 1623 Folio Edition

Shakespeare Made Easy

Titles in the series
Macbeth
Julius Caesar
The Merchant of Venice
Romeo and Juliet
Henry IV Part One
A Midsummer Night's Dream
Twelfth Night
The Tempest
King Lear
Hamlet
Othello
Henry V

Contents

Introduction

Shakespeare Made Easy is intended for readers approaching the plays for the first time, who find the language of Elizabethan poetic drama an initial obstacle to understanding and enjoyment. In the past, the only answer to the problem has been to grapple with the difficulties with the aid of explanatory footnotes (often missing when they are most needed) and a stern teacher. Generations of students have complained that 'Shakespeare was ruined for me at school'.

Usually a fuller appreciation of Shakespeare's plays comes in later life, when the mind has matured and language skills are more developed. Often the desire to read Shakespeare for pleasure and enrichment follows from a visit to the theatre, where excellence of acting and production can bring to life qualities which sometimes lie dormant on the printed page.

Shakespeare Made Easy can never be a substitute for the original plays. It cannot possibly convey the full meaning of Shakespeare's poetic expression, which is untranslatable. *Shakespeare Made Easy* concentrates on the dramatic aspect, enabling the novice to become familiar with the plot and characters, and to experience one facet of Shakespeare's genius. To know and understand the central issues of each play is a sound starting point for further exploration and development.

Discretion can be used in choosing the best method to employ. One way is to read the original Shakespeare first, ignoring the modern translation or using it only when interest or understanding flags. Another way is to read the translation first, to establish confidence and familiarity with plots and characters.

Either way, cross-reference can be illuminating. The modern text can explain 'what is being said' if Shakespeare's language is particularly complex or his expression antiquated. The Shakespeare text will show the reader of the modern paraphrase how much more can be expressed in poetry than in prose.

The use of *Shakespeare Made Easy* means that the newcomer need never be overcome by textual difficulties. From first to last, a measure of understanding is at hand – the key is provided for what has been a locked door to many students in the past. And as understanding grows, so an awareness develops of the potential of language as a vehicle for philosophic and moral expression, beauty, and the abidingly memorable.

Even professional Shakespearian scholars can never hope to arrive at a complete understanding of the plays. Each critic, researcher, actor or producer merely adds a little to the work that has already been done, or makes fresh interpretations of the texts for new generations. For everyone, Shakespearian appreciation is a journey. *Shakespeare Made Easy* is intended to help with the first steps.

In the words of Dr Johnson (*Preface to Shakespeare*, 1756): 'I hope I have made my author's meaning accessible to many who before were frightened from perusing him.'

Alan Durband

William Shakespeare

His life

William Shakespeare was born in Stratford-on-Avon, Warwickshire, on 23 April 1564, the son of a prosperous wool and leather merchant. Very little is known of his early life. From parish records we know that he married Ann Hathaway in 1582, when he was eighteen, and she was twenty-six. They had three children, the eldest of whom died in childhood.

Between his marriage and the next thing we know about him, there is a gap of ten years. Probably he became a member of a travelling company of actors. By 1592 he had settled in London, and had earned a reputation as an actor and playwright.

Theatres were then in their infancy. The first (called *The Theatre*) was built by the actor James Burbage in 1576, in Shoreditch, then a suburb of London. Two more followed as the taste for theatre grew: *The Curtain* in 1577 and *The Rose* in 1587. The demand for new plays naturally increased. Shakespeare probably earned a living adapting old plays and working in collaboration with others on new ones. Today we would call him a 'freelance', since he was not permanently attached to one theatre.

In 1594, a new company of actors, The Lord Chamberlain's Men was formed, and Shakespeare was one of the shareholders. He remained a member throughout his working life. The Company was regrouped in 1603, and re-named The King's Men, with James I as their patron.

Shakespeare and his fellow-actors prospered. In 1598 they built their own theatre, *The Globe*, which broke away from the traditional rectangular shape of the inn and its yard (the early home of travelling bands of actors). Shakespeare described it in *Henry V* as 'this wooden O', because it was circular.

Many other theatres were built by investors eager to profit from the new enthusiasm for drama. *The Hope, The Fortune, The Red Bull,* and *The Swan* were all open-air 'public' theatres. There were also many 'private' (or indoor) theatres, one of which (*The Blackfriars*) was purchased by Shakespeare and his friends because the child actors who performed there were dangerous competitors (Shakespeare denounces them in *Hamlet*).

After writing some thirty-seven plays (the exact number is something which scholars argue about), Shakespeare retired to his native Stratford, wealthy and respected. He died on his birthday, in 1616.

His plays

Shakespeare's plays were not all published in his lifetime. None of them comes to us exactly as he wrote it.

In Elizabethan times, plays were not regarded as either literature or good reading matter. They were written at speed (often by more than one writer), performed perhaps ten or twelve times, and then discarded. Fourteen of Shakespeare's plays were first printed in Quarto (17cm × 21cm) volumes, not all with his name as the author. Some were authorized (the 'good' Quartos) and probably were printed from prompt copies provided by the theatre. Others were pirated (the 'bad' Quartos) by booksellers who may have employed shorthand writers, or bought actors' copies after the run of the play had ended.

In 1623, seven years after Shakespeare's death, John Hemming and Henry Condell (fellow-actors and shareholders in The King's Men) published a collected edition of Shakespeare's works – thirty-six plays in all – in a Folio (21cm × 34cm) edition. From their introduction it would seem that they used Shakespeare's original manuscripts ('we have scarce received from him a blot in his papers') but the Folio volumes that still survive are not all exactly alike, nor are the plays printed as we know them today, with act and scene divisions and stage-directions.

A modern edition of a Shakespeare play is the result of a great deal of scholarly research and editorial skill over several centuries. The aim is always to publish a text (based on the good and bad Quartos and the Folio editions) that most closely resembles what Shakespeare intended. Misprints have added to the problems, so some words and lines are pure guesswork. This explains why some versions of Shakespeare's plays differ from others.

His theatre

The first purpose-built playhouse in Elizabethan London, constructed in 1576, was *The Theatre*. Its co-founders were John Brayne, an investor, and James Burbage, a carpenter turned actor. Like the six or seven 'public' (or outdoor) theatres which followed it over the next thirty years, it was situated outside the city, to avoid conflict with the authorities. They disapproved of players and playgoing, partly on moral and political grounds, and partly because of the danger of spreading the plague. (There were two major epidemics during Shakespeare's lifetime, and on each occasion the theatres were closed for lengthy periods.)

The Theatre was a financial success, and Shakespeare's company performed there until 1598, when a dispute over the lease of the land forced Burbage to take down the building. It was recreated in Southwark, as *The Globe*, with Shakespeare and several of his fellow-actors as the principal shareholders.

By modern standards, *The Globe* was small. Externallly, the octagonal building measured less than thirty metres across, but in spite of this it could accommodate an audience of between two and three thousand people. (The largest of the

Interior of the Swan Theatre – from a pen and ink drawing made in 1596 (Mansell Collection)

three theatres at the National Theatre complex in London today seats 1160.)

Performances were advertised by means of playbills posted around the city, and they took place during the hours of daylight when the weather was suitable. A flag flew to show that all was well, to save playgoers a wasted journey.

At the entrance, a doorkeeper collected one penny (about 60p in modern money) for admission to the 'pit' – a name taken from the old inn-yards, where bear-baiting and cock-fighting were popular sports. This was the minimum charge for seeing a play. The 'groundlings', as they were called, simply stood around the three sides of the stage, in the open air. Those who were better off could pay extra for a seat under cover. Stairs led from the pit to three tiers of galleries round the walls. The higher one went, the more one paid. The best seats cost one shilling, (or £6 today). In theatres owned by speculators like Francis Langley and Philip Henslowe, half the gallery takings went to the landlord.

A full house might consist of 800 groundlings and 1500 in the galleries, with a dozen more exclusive seats on the stage itself for the gentry. A new play might run for between six and sixteen performances; the average was about ten. As there were no breaks between scenes, and no intervals, most plays could be performed in two hours. A trumpet sounded three times before the play began.

The acting company assembled in the Tiring House at the rear of the stage. This was where they 'attired' (or dressed) themselves: not in costumes representing the period of the play, but in Elizabethan doublet and hose. All performances were therefore in modern dress, though no expense was spared to make the stage costumes lavish. The entire company was male. By law actresses were not allowed, and female roles were performed by boys.

Access to the stage from the Tiring House was through two doors, one on each side of the stage. Because there was no front curtain, every entrance had to have its corresponding exit, so an actor killed on stage had to be carried off. There was no scenery: the audience used its imagination, guided by the spoken word. Storms and night scenes might well be performed on sunny days in mid-afternoon; the Elizabethan playgoer relied entirely on the playwrights' descriptive skills to establish the dramatic atmosphere.

Once on stage, the actors and their expensive clothes were protected from sudden showers by a canopy, the underside of which was painted blue, and spangled with stars to represent the heavens. A trapdoor in the stage made ghostly entrances and the gravedigging scene in *Hamlet* possible. Behind the main stage, in between the two entrance doors, there was a curtained area, concealing a small inner stage, useful for bedroom scenes. Above this was a balcony, which served for castle walls (as in *Henry V*) or a domestic balcony (as in the famous scene in *Romeo and Juliet*).

The acting style in Elizabethan times was probably more declamatory than we favour today, but the close proximity of the audience also made a degree of intimacy possible. In those days soliloquies and asides seemed quite natural. Act and scene divisions did not exist (those in printed versions of the play today have been added by editors), but Shakespeare often indicates a scene-ending by a rhyming couplet.

A company such as The King's Men at *The Globe* would consist of around twenty-five actors, half of whom might be shareholders, and the rest part-timers engaged for a particular play. Amongst the shareholders in *The Globe* were several specialists – William Kempe, for example, was a renowned comedian and Robert Armin was a singer and dancer. Playwrights wrote parts to suit the actors who were available, and devised ways of overcoming the absence of women. Shakespeare often has his heroines dress as young men, and physical contact between lovers was formal compared with the realism we expect today.

His verse

Shakespeare wrote his plays mostly in blank verse: that is, unrhymed lines consisting of ten syllables, alternately stressed and unstressed. The technical term for this form is the 'iambic pentameter'. When Shakespeare first began to write for the stage, it was fashionable to maintain this regular beat from the first line of the play till the last.

Shakespeare conformed at first, and then experimented. Some of his early plays contain whole scenes in rhyming couplets – in *Romeo and Juliet*, for example, there is extensive use of rhyme, and as if to show his versatility, Shakespeare even inserts a sonnet into the dialogue.

But as he matured, he sought greater freedom of expression than rhyme allowed. Rhyme is still used to indicate a scene-ending, or to stress lines which he wishes the audience to remember. Generally, though, Shakespeare moved towards the rhythms of everyday speech. This gave him many dramatic advantages, which he fully and subtly exploits in terms of atmosphere, character, emotion, stress and pace.

It is Shakespeare's poetic imagery, however, that most distinguishes his verse from that of lesser playwrights. It enables him to stretch the imagination, express complex thought-patterns in memorable language, and convey a number of associated ideas in a compressed and economical form. A study of Shakespeare's imagery – especially in his later plays – is often the key to a full understanding of his meaning and purposes.

At the other extreme is prose. Shakespeare normally reserves it for servants, clowns, commoners, and pedestrian matters such as lists, messages and letters.

Henry V

Date

Henry V is thought to have been written in 1599. In March of that year the Earl of Essex went to Ireland to suppress a rebellion, with all the high expectations voiced by the Chorus before Act Five. By September, the Earl had returned to London in disgrace. We must assume that Shakespeare wrote *Henry V* during the intervening period.

Sources

The Chronicles of England, Scotland and Ireland, written by Raphael Holinshed in 1577, provided Shakespeare with all the basic material he needed for his history plays. Sometimes his borrowings are very close: for example, he merely translates Holinshed's prose into blank verse in the scene in which the Archbishop explains the Salic Law, and justifies the king's excursion into France. But in every other respect Shakespeare takes great liberties with history. In crafting *Henry V* he simplifies events, compresses time, invents new characters, omits important historical detail, and adds fictitious episodes. He may also have read Edward Hall's *The Union of the Noble and Illustrious Families of Lancaster and York* (published in 1548), and he certainly incorporated ideas he found in an earlier play called *The Famous Victories of Henry V* (1594, author unknown), in particular the wooing of Katherine and the episode of the Dauphin's scornful gift of tennis balls.

Text

A Quarto edition of the play, probably prepared by actors who had performed in it, appeared in 1600 and was reprinted in 1602 and 1619. In 1623, Hemming and Condell published their Folio version, almost certainly from an original manuscript in Shakespeare's own hand. A modern edition of *Henry V* is usually based on this Folio text, though the first Quarto is useful in identifying and correcting errors and omissions, often the fault of the compositors who set up the type. There is therefore no definitive text of *Henry V*. As a practical man of the theatre, Shakespeare would make changes in his first draft to suit the size of his acting company, so a minor character might appear in one edition but not another, or have a different name, or be listed as one of the characters yet be given no lines to say. Every editor, therefore, is faced with choices, and (as always) experts disagree: no two editions are exactly alike. In this one, spelling and punctuation have been modernised throughout, in order to remove unnecessary and pedantic obstacles to a full enjoyment of the play.

The historical background

Eight of Shakespeare's history plays cover English history from the reign of Richard II through to the accession of Henry VII. *Henry V* is the fourth play in the cycle.

In the first play, *Richard II*, a weak King is deposed and murdered at the instigation of his cousin Henry Bolingbroke, Duke of Lancaster, who reigns over a troubled kingdom as Henry IV. Because he had usurped the throne Henry IV lived in constant danger from the nobles who had helped his rise to power. *Henry IV Part One* and *Henry IV Part Two* cover his strife-torn reign, with his son Prince Hal depicted as an irresponsible young ne'er-do-well with a taste for low-life companions and revelry. None of the rebellions against Henry

IV succeeded, and on his death Prince Hal is crowned as Henry V. Shakespeare's play shows how the new and wholly reformed king unites his country and fights a patriotic and successful war against the French, the justification for which is traced back to Henry's great-grandfather, Edward III, whose mother was Isabella, daughter of Philip IV of France. The French denied his claim on the grounds that the Salic Law forbade succession through the female line. No mention is made in the play of the historical fact that Edward III had renounced his claim to the throne in 1360, over 50 years before Henry V revived it.

Henry V

Original text and modern version

The characters

Chorus
Henry the Fifth   King of England
Duke of Gloucester ⎱
Duke of Clarence   ⎰ his brothers
Duke of Exeter   his uncle
Duke of York   his cousin
Duke of Bedford
Earl of Salisbury
Earl of Westmorland
Earl of Warwick
Archbishop of Canterbury
Bishop of Ely
Richard, Earl of Cambridge ⎫
Henry, Lord Scroop of Masham ⎬ traitors
Sir Thomas Grey ⎭
Pistol ⎫
Nym ⎬ formerly **Falstaff's** companions
Bardolph ⎭
Boy   formerly **Falstaff's** page
Hostess   formerly **Mistress Quickly**, now **Pistol's** wife
Sir Thomas Erpingham
Captain Gower   an Englishman
Captain Fluellen   a Welshman
Captain MacMorris   an Irishman
Captain Jamy   a Scot
John Bates ⎫
Alexander Court ⎬ English soldiers
Michael Williams ⎭
Herald
Charles the Sixth   King of France
Isabel   his Queen
The Dauphin   their son

Katherine   their daughter
Alice   Katherine's lady-in-waiting
The Constable of France
Duke of Britaine ⎫
Duke of Orleans ⎪
Lord Rambures ⎬   French noblemen at Agincourt
Lord Grandpré ⎪
Duke of Burgundy ⎭
Montjoy   the French Herald
Governor of Harfleur
French Ambassadors   to England
French Soldier

Prologue

Enter **Chorus**

Chorus Oh for a muse of fire, that would ascend
The brightest heaven of invention:
A kingdom for a stage, princes to act,
And monarchs to behold the swelling scene!
5   Then should the warlike Harry, like himself,
Assume the port of Mars; and at his heels,
Leashed in like hounds, should famine, sword, and fire
Crouch for employment. But pardon, gentles all,
The flat unraised spirits that hath dared
10 On this unworthy scaffold to bring forth
So great an object. Can this cockpit hold
The vasty fields of France? Or may we cram
Within this wooden O the very casques
That did affright the air at Agincourt?
15 Oh pardon! Since a crooked figure may
Attest in little place a million,
And let us, ciphers to this great account,
On your imaginary forces work.
Suppose within the girdle of these walls
20 Are now confined two mighty monarchies,
Whose high upreared and abutting fronts
The perilous narrow ocean parts asunder.
Piece out our imperfections with your thoughts:
Into a thousand parts divide one man,
25 And make imaginary puissance.
Think, when we talk of horses, that you see them
Printing their proud hoofs i'th' receiving earth;
For 'tis your thoughts that now must deck our kings,
Carry them here and there, jumping o'er times,

The Prologue

*An **Announcer** addresses the audience before the play begins.*

Announcer   Oh, for the gift of fiery inspiration, to reach the topmost heights of creativity! My stage would be a kingdom. My actors, real princes. My audience, monarchs, to behold the awe-inspiring spectacle. Then the martial King Harry, a natural for the role, would play the part of Mars, [*the god of war*]. Famine, bloodshed and fire, held on a leash like dogs, would crouch at his heels, waiting for work. But, ladies and gentlemen, forgive the feeble, uninspiring players who dare to enact so great a matter on this inadequate stage. Can this theatre accommodate the vast acreage of France? Or can we cram within its walls the fighting men who made Agincourt so terrifying? My apologies! However, since one and a few noughts can mean 'a million', permit us – mere nobodies in the sum total of this great business – to get to work on your imaginations . . . Suppose that within the perimeter of these walls two mighty kingdoms are enclosed, whose cliff-lined coasts are divided by a dangerous and narrow sea . . . Make good our shortcomings with your thoughts. Pretend that each man represents a thousand, and create an imaginary army. When we talk of horses, visualize them proudly stamping their hoof-prints in the soft ground . . . Because – it's your thoughts now that must enrobe our kings. Give them free rein, skipping over periods of time and condensing the

30   Turning th'accomplishment of many years
      Into an hourglass – for the which supply,
      Admit me Chorus to this history.
      Who, Prologue-like, your humble patience pray
      Gently to hear, kindly to judge, our play.

                                                    [Exit

happenings of many years into the span of a single hour. To help generate them, let me be your compere in this drama. As such, may I humbly request that you listen to our play courteously, and criticise it in a kindly way.

[*He bows, and leaves. The play begins*]

Act one

Scene 1

London. An antechamber in the King's palace. Enter the
Archbishop of Canterbury *and the* **Bishop of Ely.**

Canterbury My lord, I'll tell you. That self bill is urged
    Which in the eleventh year of the last king's reign
    Was like, and had indeed against us passed,
    But that the scrambling and unquiet time
5   Did push it out of farther question.

Ely But how, my lord, shall we resist it now?

Canterbury It must be thought on. If it pass against us,
    We lose the better half of our possession,
    For all the temporal lands which men devout
10   By testament have given to the Church
    Would they strip from us; being valued thus:
    As much as would maintain, to the King's honour,
    Full fifteen earls and fifteen hundred knights,
    Six thousand and two hundred good esquires;
15   And, to relief of lazars and weak age,
    Of indigent faint souls past corporal toil,
    A hundred almshouses right well supplied:
    And to the coffers of the King, beside,
    A thousand pounds by the year. Thus runs the bill.

20 **Ely** This would drink deep.

Canterbury 'Twould drink the cup and all.

Ely But what prevention?

Act one

Scene 1

*London. A room in the royal palace. The **Archbishop of Canterbury** and **The Bishop of Ely** enter, deep in conversation.*

Canterbury   My lord, let me tell you this. The very bill is being put through Parliament that in the eleventh year of King Henry's reign might well have been passed against us – and would indeed have been passed, had not the troubled times precluded further discussion.

Ely   But how, my lord, can we oppose it now?

Canterbury   We've got to think about it. If it's passed against us, we'll lose more than half our property, because they'll strip us of all the secular land which pious men have bequeathed to the Church. It would amount to this: the cost of maintaining in honour of the King fully fifteen earls; fifteen hundred knights; six thousand two hundred apprentice knights; a hundred well-endowed almshouses for the relief of lepers, the elderly, and sick paupers incapable of work; as well as putting a thousand pounds a year into the King's exchequer. That's what the bill would be!

Ely   This would drain us.

Canterbury   Cup and all!

Ely   How can we stop it?

Act one   Scene 1

Canterbury   The King is full of grace and fair regard.

Ely   And a true lover of the holy Church.

25 **Canterbury**   The courses of his youth promised it not.
The breath no sooner left his father's body
But that his wildness, mortified in him,
Seemed to die too. Yea, at that very moment
Consideration like an angel came
30 And whipped the offending Adam out of him,
Leaving his body as a paradise
T'envelop and contain celestial spirits.
Never was such a sudden scholar made;
Never came reformation in a flood
35 With such a heady currance scouring faults;
Nor never Hydra-headed wilfulness
So soon did lose his seat – and all at once –
As in this king.

Ely   We are blessed in the change.

40 **Canterbury**   Hear him but reason in divinity
And, all-admiring, with an inward wish
You would desire the King were made a prelate;
Hear him debate of commonwealth affairs,
You would say it hath been all-in-all his study;
45 List his discourse of war, and you shall hear
A fearful battle rendered you in music;
Turn him to any cause of policy,
The Gordian knot of it he will unloose,
Familiar as his garter; that when he speaks,
50 The air, a chartered libertine, is still,
And the mute wonder lurketh in men's ears
To steel his sweet and honeyed sentences
So that the art and practic part of life
Must be the mistress to this theoric,
55 Which is a wonder how his grace should glean it,

Canterbury   The King is gracious and means well.

Ely   And a true lover of the holy Church.

Canterbury   His youthful behaviour showed no sign
of it, but the breath had no sooner left his father's
body than his wildness, destroyed within him,
seemed to die too. Yes: at that very moment self-
awareness, like an angel, came and whipped the
wickedness out of him, leaving his body like a
paradise suitable for hosting heavenly qualities.
Never did a man become a scholar so suddenly;
never did reformation come in such a torrent as to
sweep away all faults; nor was misbehaviour in its
many forms so soon dislodged, and all at once, as
in the case of this King.

Ely   The change is a blessing to us.

Canterbury   Just hear him discuss theology, and, full
of admiration, you would mentally wish he could be
made a bishop. Hear him in political debate, and
you would say it was his speciality. Listen to him on
the subject of war, and you'd hear the sweet music
of a military strategist. Put any complicated political
issue to him, and he'll undo the knots as easily as
he takes off his garter. When he speaks, the air —
though free to move about — is still, and men in
silent wonderment listen to his dulcet utterances.
Practical experience must be behind this theory, but
it's astonishing how his grace acquired it, since his

Since his addiction was to courses vain,
His companies unlettered, rude, and shallow,
His hours filled up with riots, banquets, sports,
And never noted in him any study,
60   Any retirement, any sequestration
From open haunts and popularity.

Ely   The strawberry grows underneath the nettle,
And wholesome berries thrive and ripen best
Neighboured by fruit of baser quality;
65   And so the Prince obscured his contemplation
Under the veil of wildness; which, no doubt,
Grew like the summer grass, fastest by night,
Unseen, yet crescive in his faculty.

Canterbury   It must be so, for miracles are ceased;
70   And therefore we must needs admit the means
How things are perfected.

Ely   But, my good lord,
How now for mitigation of this bill
Urged by the Commons? Doth his majesty
75   Incline to it, or no?

Canterbury   He seems indifferent,
Or rather swaying more upon our part
Than cherishing the exhibiters against us;
For I have made an offer to his majesty –
80   Upon our spiritual convocation
And in regard of causes now in hand,
Which I have opened to his grace at large –
As touching France, to give a greater sum
Than ever at one time the clergy yet
85   Did to his predecessors part withal.

Ely   How did this offer seem received, my lord?

inclination was towards worthless things; his companions illiterate, ill-mannered and shallow-minded; his time preoccupied with debauchery, feasting and merrymaking. There was never any sign in him of studiousness, of reticence, or dislike for common society and popularity.

Ely   Strawberries grow beneath nettles. Healthy berries thrive and ripen best when they have inferior fruit as neighbours. So Prince Henry concealed his serious side beneath a veil of wild behaviour. No doubt, it grew like the grass does in summer: fastest in the dark, when unseen; but constantly developing by its very nature.

Canterbury   It must be so; the days of miracles have ceased. Therefore we must accept that there are stages in reaching perfection.

Ely   But, my good lord, what chance is there of watering down this Act the Commons want to pass? Does his majesty favour it, or not?

Canterbury   He seems impartial, or perhaps leaning towards us more than towards the bill's sponsors. I have made an offer to his Majesty – on behalf of the Synod, and with regard to current issues which I have discussed with his Grace at length – concerning France. It is to give him a larger donation than the clergy ever gave to his predecessors at any one time.

Ely   How did he react to this offer, my lord?

31

Canterbury   With good acceptance of his majesty,
    Save that there was not time enough to hear,
    As I perceived his grace would fain have done,
90   The severals and unhidden passages
    Of his true titles to some certain dukedoms,
    And generally to the crown and seat of France,
    Derived from Edward, his great-grandfather.

Ely   What was the impediment that broke this off?

95 **Canterbury**   The French ambassador upon that instant
    Craved audience; and the hour I think is come
    To give him hearing. Is it four o'clock?

Ely   It is.

Canterbury   Then go we in, to know his embassy;
100   Which I could with a ready guess declare
    Before the Frenchman speak a word of it.

Ely   I'll wait upon you, and I long to hear it.

[Exeunt

Scene 2

London. The presence chamber in the King's palace. Enter
King Henry, *the* **Dukes of Gloucester, Bedford,** *and*
Exeter, *and the* **Earls of Warwick** *and* **Westmorland.**

King Henry   Where is my gracious lord of Canterbury?

Exeter   Not here in presence.

King Henry   Send for him, good uncle.

Canterbury   His Majesty took it well, except there wasn't sufficient time for him to hear – as a I realized his Grace would have wished – the details of his valid claims to certain Dukedoms, and the throne of France, descending from Edward, his great-grandfather.

Ely   What interrupted you?

Canterbury   Right then the French ambassador requested an audience – and now is the time, I think, for him to be heard. Is it four o'clock?

Ely   It is.

Canterbury   Then let us go in to hear his message, which I can guess before the Frenchman speaks a word of it.

Ely   I'll join you, and look forward to hearing it.

[*They go*]

Scene 2

London. The throne room in the royal palace. Enter **King Henry V,** *the* **Dukes of Gloucester, Bedford** *and* **Exeter,** *attended.*

King Henry   Where is my gracious lord of Canterbury?

Exeter   He's not present.

King Henry   Send for him, good uncle. [**Exeter** *signals to an* **Attendant**]

Westmorland   Shall we call in the ambassador, my liege?

5 **King Henry**   Not yet, my cousin. We would be resolved,
   Before we hear him, of some things of weight
   That task our thoughts, concerning us and France.

[*Enter the* **Archbishop of Canterbury** *and the* **Bishop of Ely**]

Canterbury   God and his angels guard your sacred throne,
   And make you long become it!

10 **King Henry**   Sure we thank you.
   My learned lord, we pray you to proceed,
   And justly and religiously unfold
   Why the law Salic that they have in France
   Or should or should not bar us in our claim.
15 And God forbid, my dear and faithful lord,
   That you should fashion, wrest, or bow your reading,
   Or nicely charge your understanding soul
   With opening titles miscreate, whose right
   Suits not in native colours with the truth;
20 For God doth know how many now in health
   Shall drop their blood in approbation
   Of what your reverence shall incite us to.
   Therefore take heed how you impawn our person,
   How you awake our sleeping sword of war;
25 We charge you in the name of God, take heed.
   For never two such kingdoms did contend
   Without much fall of blood, whose guiltless drops
   Are every one a woe, a sore complaint
   'Gainst him whose wrongs gives edge unto the swords
30 That makes such waste in brief mortality.
   Under this conjuration speak, my lord,
   For we will hear, note, and believe in heart
   That what you speak is in your conscience washed
   As pure as sin with baptism.

Westmorland   Shall we call in the Ambassador, Your
Majesty?

King Henry   Not yet, cousin. Before we hear him, we
would like the answers to some weightier matters
that are on our mind, concerning us and France.

[*The* **Archbishop of Canterbury** *and the* **Bishop of
Ely** *enter*]

Canterbury   God and His angels guard your sacred
throne, and may you long grace it!

King Henry   Assuredly we thank you. My learned lord,
pray continue, and explain on legal and religious
grounds why the Salic Law they have in France
does – or does not – exclude us in our claim. And
God forbid, my dear and loyal lord, that you should
distort, twist, or bias your interpretation; or
compromise your integrity by advocating
illegitimate claims, the rights of which do not
accord with the truth. Because God alone knows
how many healthy men will shed their blood to
validate whatever claim your reverence may
encourage us to pursue. Therefore, think carefully
before you implicate our royal self, and stir us to
war; in God's name, take care. Never did two such
kingdoms fight without great loss of blood; each
innocent drop a sorrow, a grievous reproach to the
one whose cause sharpens the swords that wreak
the slaughter. With this proviso, speak, my lord; we
shall hear, note, and sincerely believe that what you
say is as sin-free as the soul after baptism.

35 **Canterbury**   Then hear me, gracious sovereign, and you
          peers
       That owe your selves, your lives, and services
       To this imperial throne. There is no bar
       To make against your highness' claim to France
40   But this, which they produce from Pharamond:
       'In terram Salicam mulieres ne succedant' –
       'No woman shall succeed in Salic land' –
       Which Salic land the French unjustly gloze
       To be the realm of France, and Pharamond
45   The founder of this law and female bar.
       Yet their own authors faithfully affirm
       That the land Salic is in Germany,
       Between the floods of Sala and of Elbe,
       Where Charles the Great, having subdued the Saxons,
50   There left behind and settled certain French
       Who, holding in disdain the German women
       For some dishonest manners of their life,
       Established then this law: to wit, no female
       Should be inheritrix in Salic land;
55   Which Salic, as I said, 'twixt Elbe and Sala,
       Is at this day in Germany called Meissen.
       Then doth it well appear the Salic Law
       Was not devised for the realm of France;
       Nor did the French possess the Salic land
60   Until four hundred one-and-twenty years
       After defunction of King Pharamond,
       Idly supposed the founder of this law,
       Who died within the year of our redemption
       Four hundred twenty-six; and Charles the Great
65   Subdued the Saxons, and did seat the French
       Beyond the river Sala, in the year
       Eight hundred five. Besides, their writers say,
       King Pepin, which deposed Childeric,
       Did, as heir general, being descended

Canterbury   Then hear me, gracious sovereign, and you lords who owe your selves, your lives and your duties to this imperial throne. There is no bar to Your Highness's claim to France, except this, which they quote from the laws of King Pharamond: 'In terram Salicam, mulieres ne succedant'; meaning 'Women are excluded from succession to the throne in Salic Land'. This 'Salic Land' the French wrongly interpret to be the realm of France, with Pharamond the originator of this law about barring females. Yet their own historians positively state that Salic Land is in Germany, between the rivers Sala and the Elbe, where Charlemagne (after defeating the Saxons) left behind a colony of Frenchmen. Having no respect for German women on account of their promiscuous ways, they then established this law: that is to say, that no female should succeed in Salic Land (which place, as I said, is between the Elbe and Sala rivers, and today known in Germany as Meissen). From this it is quite clear that the Salic Law was not devised for the realm of France, nor did the French possess the Salic Land until four hundred and twenty-one years after King Pharamond (rashly regarded as the founder of this law) died in 426 AD. Charlemagne conquered the Saxons and established the French beyond the River Sala, in 805. Besides, their historians say that King Pepin (who overthrew King Childeric) as the

70   Of Blithild, which was daughter to King Clothaire,
      Made claim and title to the crown of France.
      Hugh Capet also, who usurped the crown
      Of Charles the Duke of Lorraine, sole heir male
      Of the true line and stock of Charles the Great,
75   To fine his title with some shows of truth,
      Though in pure truth it was corrupt and naught,
      Conveyed himself as heir to the Lady Lingard,
      Daughter to Charlemain, who was the son
      To Louis the emperor, and Louis the son
80   Of Charles the Great. Also, King Louis the Ninth,
      Who was sole heir to the usurper Capet,
      Could not keep quiet in his conscience,
      Wearing the crown of France, till satisfied
      That fair Queen Isabel, his grandmother,
85   Was lineal of the Lady Ermengare,
      Daughter to Charles, the foresaid Duke of Lorraine;
      By the which marriage the line of Charles the Great
      Was reunited to the crown of France.
      So that, as clear as is the summer's sun,
90   King Pepin's title and Hugh Capet's claim,
      King Louis his satisfaction, all appear
      To hold in right and title of the female;
      So do the kings of France unto this day,
      Howbeit they would hold up this Salic Law
95   To bar your highness claiming from the female,
      And rather choose to hide them in a net
      Than amply to embar their crooked titles,
      Usurped from you and your progenitors.

      King Henry   May I with right and conscience make this
100   claim?

      Canterbury   The sin upon my head, dread sovereign!
      For in the Book of Numbers is it writ,
      'When the man dies, let the inheritance

rightful heir (being descended from Queen Blithild, who was King Clotaire's daughter) made claim to the crown of France. So did Hugh Capet (who usurped the crown of Duke Charles of Lorraine, the sole male heir of the true lineage of Charlemagne); and to back his case with some plausible facts (though undeniably it was unsound and worthless), he staked his claim as heir to Lady Lingard, daughter of Charles the Second, the son of the Emperor Louis, himself the son of Charlemagne. Also, King Louis the Ninth, (who was sole heir to the usurper Hugh Capet), could not sleep in peace as King of France till he was satisfied that fair Queen Isabel, his grandmother, was a descendant of Lady Ermengard, daughter of the aforesaid Duke Charles of Lorraine, by which marriage the line of Charlemagne was reunited with the crown of France. So that – as clear as daylight – King Pepin's title, and Hugh Capet's claim, and King Louis's grounds for peace of mind, all appear to uphold the principle of female inheritance. So do the kings of France to this day, much as they would cite the Salic Law to bar Your Highness from claiming through the female line. They prefer hiding behind this flimsy cover to exposing their own invalid claims to a throne which they've usurped from you and your predecessors.

King Henry   [*seeking a simple answer to a simple question*] May I make this claim legitimately and with a clear conscience?

Canterbury   I take full responsibility for it, my revered sovereign. In the Book of Numbers it is written: 'When the son dies, the inheritance passes to the

Descend unto the daughter'. Gracious lord,
105 Stand for your own; unwind your bloody flag;
Look back into your mighty ancestors.
Go, my dread lord, to your great-grandsire's tomb,
From whom you claim; invoke his warlike spirit,
And your great-uncle's, Edward the Black Prince,
110 Who on the French ground played a tragedy,
Making defeat on the full power of France,
While his most mighty father on a hill
Stood smiling to behold his lion's whelp
Forage in blood of French nobility.
115 Oh noble English, that could entertain
With half their forces the full pride of France,
And let another half stand laughing by,
All out of work, and cold for action!

Ely Awake remembrance of those valiant dead,
120 And with your puissant arm renew their feats.
You are their heir, you sit upon their throne,
The blood and courage that renowned them
Runs in your veins; and my thrice-puissant liege
Is in the very May-morn of his youth,
125 Ripe for exploits and mighty enterprises.

Exeter Your brother kings and monarchs of the earth
Do all expect that you should rouse yourself
As did the former lions of your blood.

Westmorland They know your grace hath cause, and
130   means and might;
So hath your highness. Never king of England
Had nobles richer and more loyal subjects,
Whose hearts have left their bodies here in England
And lie pavilioned in the fields of France.

135 **Canterbury** Oh let their bodies follow, my dear liege,
With blood and sword and fire, to win your right!

daughter.' Gracious lord, stand up for your rights!
Unfurl the blood-red flag of war! Take inspiration
from your ancestors! Go, my illustrious lord, to the
tomb of your great-grandfather, from whom you
base your claim. Invoke his militant spirit, and that
of your great-uncle, Edward the Black Prince, who
played a dramatic role on French territory, defeating
the entire French army while his most mighty father
stood smiling on a hilltop as he beheld his
lionhearted son ravage the French nobility. Oh,
noble Englishmen, to take on the full might of
France with only half their forces, letting the other
half stand by – laughing, out of work, and cold from
lack of action!

Ely   Remember anew those valiant dead, and with
your strong arm repeat their achievements! You are
their heir; you sit upon their throne; the blood and
courage that made them renowned runs through
your veins: and my three-ways-justified sovereign is
in his youthful prime, ripe for valorous deeds and
mighty enterprises!

Exeter   Your brother kings and monarchs throughout
the world all expect you to rouse yourself like your
lion-hearted ancestors!

Westmorland   They know Your Grace has a valid
cause, the finance and the military might: so indeed
your highness has! No king of England ever had
richer nobles, or more loyal subjects, whose hearts
have left their bodies here in England and now lie
encamped upon the fields of France!

Canterbury   Oh, let their bodies follow, my dear liege,
with blood and sword and fire, to win what's yours

In aid whereof, we of the spiritualty
Will raise your highness such a mighty sum
As never did the clergy at one time
140   Bring in to any of your ancestors.

King Henry We must not only arm to invade the French
But lay down our proportions to defend
Against the Scot, who will make raid upon us
With all advantages.

145 **Canterbury** They of those marches, gracious sovereign,
Shall be a wall sufficient to defend
Our inland from the pilfering borderers.

King Henry We do not mean the coursing snatchers only
But fear the main intendment of the Scot,
150   Who hath been still a giddy neighbour to us.
For you shall read that my great-grandfather
Never went with his forces into France
But that the Scot on his unfurnished kingdom
Came pouring like the tide into a breach
155   With ample and brim fullness of his force
Galling the gleaned land with hot assays,
Girding with grievous siege castles and towns,
That England, being empty of defence,
Hath shook and trembled at th'ill neighbourhood.

160 **Canterbury** She hath been then more feared than harmed,
    my liege.
For hear her but exampled by herself:
When all her chivalry hath been in France
And she a mourning widow of her nobles,
165   She hath herself not only well defended
But taken and impounded as a stray
The King of Scots, whom she did send to France
To fill King Edward's fame with prisoner kings
And make your chronicle as rich with praise

by right! In aid of this, we of the clergy will raise for your majesty a greater sum than any single contribution made by us to any of your ancestors!

King Henry   We must not only mobilise to invade the French: we must dispose our troops to defend ourselves against the Scots, who will attack us while they have the chance.

Canterbury   Those who live in the northern counties, gracious sovereign, will be a wall sufficient to defend our mainland from the thieving borderers.

King Henry   We don't just mean the raiding parties: it's the Scots as a whole we fear. They've always been an unpredictable neighbour of ours. It's an historical fact that my great-grandfather never invaded France without the Scots came pouring into his unprotected kingdom like the tide through a hole in a dyke, with massive forces harassing the undefended land with ferocious attacks, besieging castles and towns – so that England, quite defenceless, shook and trembled at the sound of it all.

Canterbury   Then she has been more frightened than hurt, my liege. Take a practical example. When all her men-at-arms were in France, and she was bereft of all her noblemen, not only did she well defend herself, she captured and impounded – like a stray animal – the King of Scotland, David the Second. She sent him to France, to enhance Edward the Third's renown as one who numbered kings amongst his prisoners, and to make her history as

170 As is the ooze and bottom of the sea
    With sunken wrack and sumless treasuries.

Westmorland   But there's a saying very old and true:
                'If that you will France win,
                Then with Scotland first begin.'
175 For once the eagle England being in prey,
    To her unguarded nest the weasel Scot
    Comes sneaking, and so sucks her princely eggs,
    Playing the mouse in absence of the cat,
    To 'tame and havoc more than she can eat.

180 **Exeter**   It follows then, the cat must stay at home.
    Yet that is but a crushed necessity,
    Since we have locks to safeguard necessaries
    And pretty traps to catch the petty thieves.
    While that the armed hand doth fight abroad,
185 Th' advised head defends itself at home.
    For government, though high and low and lower,
    Put into parts, doth keep in one consent,
    Congreeing in a full and natural close,
    Like music.

190 **Canterbury**   True. Therefore doth heaven divide
    The state of man in divers functions,
    Setting endeavour in continual motion;
    To which is fixed, as an aim or butt,
    Obedience. For so work the honey-bees,
195 Creatures that by a rule in nature teach
    The act of order to a peopled kingdom.
    They have a king, and officers of sorts,
    Where some like magistrates correct at home;
    Others like merchants venture trade abroad;
200 Others like soldiers, armed in their stings,
    Make boot upon the summer's velvet buds,
    Which pillage they with merry march bring home

rich with glory as the oozy seabed is with sunken wrecks and priceless treasure.

Westmorland   But there's a saying, very old and true:

> 'If it's France you want to win
> Then with Scotland first begin.'

Once the eagle – England – goes out seeking prey, the weasel – Scotland – sneaks into her unguarded nest, sucking the contents of her princely eggs, and acting the role of the mouse when the cat's away; breaking into and wrecking more than she can eat.

Exeter   It follows, then, that the cat must stay at home. But that's hardly necessary, since we have locks to safeguard valuables, and ingenious traps to catch petty thieves. While the country's armoured hand is fighting abroad, its canny head defends itself at home; because the state, though divided into upper, middle and lower classes, acts in unison, coming together in perfect harmony, like music.

Canterbury   True. Therefore God has given men various functions, setting in motion continuous human endeavour, the object or target of which is obedience. Honey-bees work similarly: they are creatures whose natural instincts impart a social structure to community living. They have a monarch, and officials of various kinds. Some (like magistrates) dispense the law at home; others (like merchants) venture upon trade abroad; others (like soldiers in that they have stings) plunder summer flowers, cheerfully returning home with their loot to

To the tent royal of their emperor,
Who busied in his majesty surveys
205 The singing masons building roofs of gold,
The civil citizens lading up the honey,
The poor mechanic porters crowding in
Their heavy burdens at his narrow gate,
The sad-eyed justice with his surly hum
210 Delivering o'er to executors pale
The lazy yawning drone. I this infer:
That many things, having full reference
To one consent, may work contrariously.
As many arrows loosed several ways
215 Come to one mark, as many ways meet in one town,
As many fresh streams meet in one salt sea,
As many lines close in the dial's centre,
So may a thousand actions once afoot
End in one purpose, and be all well borne
220 Without defeat. Therefore to France, my liege.
Divide your happy England into four,
Whereof take you one quarter into France,
And you withal shall make all Gallia shake.
If we with thrice such powers left at home
225 Cannot defend our own doors from the dog,
Let us be worried, and our nation lose
The name of hardiness and policy.

King Henry   Call in the messengers sent from the
Dauphin.

[Exeunt some **Attendants**

230 Now are we well resolved, and by God's help
And yours, the noble sinews of our power,
France being ours we'll bend it to our awe,
Or break it all to pieces. Or there we'll sit,
Ruling in large and ample empery
235 O'er France and all her almost kingly dukedoms,

46

the royal tent of their emperor, who, immersed in
his royal preoccupations, observes the masons
singing as they build roofs of gold; the honest
citizens loading up the honey; the poor labourers
crowding in through the narrow entrance with their
heavy burdens; the sober-faced judge with his voice
of authority, delivering the lazy, yawning drone over
to the ghastly executioners. From this I deduce that
many things that are dedicated to a common
purpose may operate divergently, just as many
arrows, shot from different spots, will converge on
one target; or many roads meet in one town; or
many freshwater streams meet in one salt sea; or
many lines converge on the centre of a sundial. In
the same way, a thousand actions, once begun,
may end in one objective, and each can be carried
out without detriment to the others. Therefore go to
France, my liege. Divide your happy England into
four. Take one quarter into France, and you will
make that country tremble. If we cannot defend our
own doors from the aggressive dog, with three
times the forces left behind at home, then we
deserve to be savaged, and our nation to lose its
reputation for daring and sound statesmanship.

King Henry   Call in the messengers sent by the
Dauphin.

[*Several* **Attendants** *leave*]

Now our mind is firmly made up. France being ours
– with God's help and yours, the noble mainstays of
our royal power – we'll make it bow to us in
obedience, or destroy it. Either we'll reign over
France and her near-royal dukedoms in total

Or lay these bones in an unworthy urn,
Tombless, with no remembrance over them.
Either our history shall with full mouth
Speak freely of our acts, or else our grave,
240 Like Turkish mute, shall have a tongueless mouth,
Not worshipped with a waxen epitaph.

[*Enter* **Ambassadors of France**, *with a tun*]

Now are we well prepared to know the pleasure
Of our fair cousin Dauphin, for we hear
Your greeting is from him, not from the King.

245 **Ambassador**   May't please your majesty to give us leave
Freely to render what we have in charge,
Or shall we sparingly show you far off
The Dauphin's meaning and our embassy?

King Henry   We are no tyrant, but a Christian king,
250 Unto whose grace our passion is as subject
As is our wretches fettered in our prisons.
Therefore with frank and with uncurbed plainness
Tell us the Dauphin's mind.

Ambassador   Thus then in few.
255 Your highness lately sending into France
Did claim some certain dukedoms, in the right
Of your great predecessor, King Edward the Third.
In answer of which claim, the Prince our master
Says that you savour too much of your youth,
260 And bids you be advised, there's naught in France
That can be with a nimble galliard won;
You cannot revel into dukedoms there.
He therefore sends you, meeter for your spirit,
This tun of treasure, and in lieu of this
265 Desires you let the dukedoms that you claim
Hear no more of you. This the Dauphin speaks.

sovereignty, or we'll lay these bones of ours in a
common grave, without a tombstone, and with no
inscription over them. Either our deeds shall be
loudly and freely proclaimed, or else our grave shall
be as voiceless as a Turkish mute, not even
dignified with a short-lived epitaph.

[**Ambassadors** *from France enter, carrying a
wooden chest*]

Now we are well prepared to know the answer of
our good friend the Dauphin, for we understand
that your greeting is from him, and not the King.

Ambassador   May it please Your Majesty to give us
permission to deliver our message frankly, or shall
we convey the Dauphin's sentiments with prudence
and discretion?

King Henry   We are no tyrant. We are a Christian
king. It follows that our emotions are as constrained
as the wretches who lie fettered in our gaols.
Therefore frankly and outspokenly tell us the
Dauphin's mind.

Ambassador   To get straight to the point. Your
Highness recently wrote to France claiming certain
dukedoms, as a descendant of your great ancestor,
King Edward the Third. In answer to that claim, my
master the Prince says that your youth is very
evident, and he would inform you that there's
nothing in France that can be gained with dancing
skills; you can't get dukedoms there through
merrymaking. He therefore sends you, as being
more appropriate to your character, this treasure-
chest; and in return he hopes there'll be no more
heard from you about the dukedoms that you claim.
This is the Dauphin's answer.

King Henry   What treasure, uncle?

Exeter   Tennis balls, my liege.

King Henry   We are glad the Dauphin is so pleasant
270   with us.
His present and your pains we thank you for.
When we have matched our rackets to these balls,
We will in France, by God's grace, play a set
Shall strike his father's crown into the hazard.
275   Tell him he hath made a match with such a wrangler
That all the courts of France will be disturbed
With chases. And we understand him well,
How he comes o'er us with our wilder days,
Not measuring what use we made of them.
280   We never valued this poor seat of England,
And therefore, living hence, did give ourself
To barbarous licence; as 'tis ever common
That men are merriest when they are from home.
But tell the Dauphin I will keep my state,
285   Be like a king, and show my sail of greatness
When I do rouse me in my throne of France;
For that I have laid by my majesty
And plodded like a man for working days.
But I will rise there with so full a glory
290   That I will dazzle all the eyes of France,
Yea strike the Dauphin blind to look on us.
And tell the pleasant Prince this mock of his
Hath turned his balls to gunstones, and his soul
Shall stand sore charged for the wasteful vengeance
295   That shall fly with them; for many a thousand widows
Shall this his mock mock out of their dear husbands,
Mock mothers from their sons, mock castles down;
Ay, some are yet ungotten and unborn
That shall have cause to curse the Dauphin's scorn.
300   But this lies all within the will of God,

King Henry   [*to* **Exeter**] What treasure is this, Uncle?

Exeter   [*opening the chest*] Tennis balls, my liege. [*In those days, tennis was a frivolous game played by fashionable young men*]

King Henry   We are glad the Dauphin has a sense of humour. We thank you for his present, and the trouble you have taken. When we've got our game together, with appropriate racquets to match these balls, by God's grace we shall, in France, play a set which will hit his father's crown into the net. Tell him he's taken on such an aggressive player that all the courts in France will resound with volleys. And we fully appreciate how he tries to put us down with references to our wilder days – not evaluating the use we made of them. We did not value this humble throne of England and therefore, living at a distance from it, we indulged in coarse pursuits; men are usually at their most frivolous when they're away from home. But tell the Dauphin that I'll stand on my royal dignity, be like a king, and show my true greatness when I take up my throne of France; that is why I put aside my royalty, and lived like a commoner. Over there I shall rise to such heights of glory that I'll dazzle everyone in France; yes – strike the Dauphin blind to look at us! And tell the witty Prince that this mockery of his has turned his tennis balls into cannon balls, and his soul will bear a heavy responsibility for the destructive vengeance that they'll cause. Many a thousand widows will mock this mock of his in terms of their dear husbands; mothers will be mocked out of their sons; castles will be mocked down. Yes, there are those as yet neither conceived nor born who'll have good reason to curse the Dauphin's scorn. But this

To whom I do appeal, and in whose name
Tell you the Dauphin I am coming on
To verge me as I may, and to put forth
My rightful hand in a well-hallowed cause.
305   So get you hence in peace. And tell the Dauphin
His jest will savour but of shallow wit
When thousands weep – more than did laugh at it.
Convey them with safe conduct. – Fare you well.

[*Exeunt* **Ambassadors**]

Exeter   This was a merry message.

310 **King Henry**   We hope to make the sender blush at it.
Therefore, my lords, omit no happy hour
That may give furth'rance to our expedition;
For we have now no thought in us but France,
Save those to God, that run before our business.
315   Therefore let our proportions for these wars
Be soon collected, and all things thought upon
That may with reasonable swiftness add
More feathers to our wings; for, God before,
We'll chide this Dauphin at his father's door.
320   Therefore let every man now task his thought,
That this fair action may on foot be brought.

[*Exeunt*]

is all subject to the will of God, to whom I appeal, and in whose name I bid you tell the Dauphin I am coming over to venge myself as well as I can, and to wield my just sword in a sacred cause. So, be gone from here in peace – and tell the Dauphin that his jest will seem a foolish one when thousands weep – more than ever laughed at it. Give them safe conduct. Fare you well.

[The **Ambassadors** *leave*]

Exeter   Such cheek!

King Henry   We hope to make the sender blush for it. Therefore, my lords, miss no opportunity to help speed our preparations, since now we think of nothing else but France: except thoughts of God, which take precedence over our affairs. Therefore let our supplies for these wars be soon collected, and everything worked out to expedite matters as quickly as possible. God willing, we'll trounce this Dauphin on his home ground: let everyone think hard so that this worthy expedition can soon begin!

[*They go*]

Act two

Chorus   Now all the youth of England are on fire,
And silken dalliance in the wardrobe lies.
Now thrive the armourers, and honour's thought
Reigns solely in the breast of every man.
5 They sell the pasture now to buy the horse,
Following the mirror of all Christian kings
With winged heels, as English Mercuries.
For now sits expectation in the air
And hides a sword from hilts unto the point
10 With crowns imperial, crowns and coronets,
Promised to Harry and his followers.
The French, advised by good intelligence
Of this most dreadful preparation,
Shake in their fear, and with pale policy
15 Seek to divert the English purposes.
Oh England! Model to thy inward greatness,
Like little body with a mighty heart,
What mightst thou do, that honour would thee do,
Were all thy children kind and natural?
20 But see, thy fault France hath in thee found out:
A nest of hollow bosoms, which he fills
With treacherous crowns; and three corrupted men –
One, Richard, Earl of Cambridge; and the second
Henry, Lord Scroop of Masham; and the third
25 Sir Thomas Grey, knight, of Northumberland –
Have, for the gilt of France – oh guilt indeed! –
Confirmed conspiracy with fearful France;
And by their hands this grace of kings must die,
If hell and treason hold their promises,

Act two

Enter the **Announcer**.

Announcer   Now all the youth of England is inspired,
and frivolous behaviour has been shelved. Now the
weapon-makers prosper, and every man thinks
solely of his honour. They sell land now to buy a
horse, hastening to follow the paragon of all
Christian kings, like so many Mercuries. [*Mercury
was the messenger of the gods*.] Now there's an
atmosphere of eager anticipation; with promise to
Harry and his followers of illustrious titles and
lavish booty to be won by the sword. The French,
advised by their expert spies of this most
threatening preparation, shake with fear, and by
subversive means attempt to change the English
plans. Oh, England! Greatness on a small scale –
like a little body with a mighty heart! What might
you aspire to, spurred on by honour, if all your
people were loving and loyal? But see. France has
detected a flaw: a nest of traitors, which it finances
with treacherous money. And three corrupted men
– first, Richard, Earl of Cambridge; second, Henry,
Lord Scroop of Masham; and third, Sir Thomas
Grey, Knight, of Northumberland – for French gold
– oh, guilt indeed! – have formed a conspiracy with
frightened France. This most gracious of kings must
die by their hands before he embarks for France, at
Southampton, if hell and treason prevail. Bear with

30 Ere he take ship for France, and in Southampton.
Linger your patience on, and we'll digest
The abuse of distance, force a play.
The sum is paid, the traitors are agreed,
The King is set from London, and the scene
35 Is now transported, gentles, to Southampton.
There is the playhouse now, there must you sit,
And thence to France shall we convey you safe,
And bring you back, charming the narrow seas
To give you gentle pass: for if we may
40 We'll not offend one stomach with our play.
But till the King come forth, and not till then,
Unto Southampton do we shift our scene.

[Exit

Scene 1

London. The Boar's Head Tavern, Eastcheap. Enter **Corporal Nym** *and* **Lieutenant Bardolph.**

Bardolph Well met, Corporal Nym.

Nym Good morrow, Lieutenant·Bardolph.

Bardolph What, are Ancient Pistol and you friends yet?

Nym For my part, I care not. I say little, but when time
5 shall serve, there shall be smiles – but that shall be as it
may. I dare not fight, but I will wink and hold out mine
iron. It is a simple one, but what though? It will toast
cheese, and it will endure cold, as another man's sword
will; and there's an end.

us, and we'll solve the travel problem and take our play a stage further. The money is paid. The traitors are agreed. The King has left London, and the scene now moves, ladies and gentlemen, to Southampton. That's where this theatre is now. There you must sit; and then we'll convey you safely to France – and bring you back! – bewitching the narrow English channel to ensure you have a calm passage. We don't want anyone throwing up because of our play! So till the King leaves, and not till then, we shift our scene to Southampton . . .

[*He goes*]

Scene 1

A street in Eastcheap, London, outside the Boar's Head Tavern. **Corporal Nym**, *a short, shaggy man with a cryptic style of speech, meets* **Lieutenant Bardolph**, *who has a fiery face and a large carbuncled nose.*

Bardolph   Greetings, Corporal Nym!

Nym   'Morning, Lieutenant Bardolph!

Bardolph   Well, are you and Ensign Pistol friends again?

Nym   Me, I don't care, I don't say much, but at the right time it'll be sorted out! But that's as maybe. Scared to fight? Well, I can close my eyes and lash out with my sword! [*He demonstrates: his sword is a short one, that looks home-made*] It's a simple one, but so what? It'll toast cheese, and face cold steel like anyone else's. 'Nuff said.

10 **Bardolph**   I will bestow a breakfast to make you friends,
and we'll be all three sworn brothers to France. Let it be
so, good Corporal Nym.

Nym   Faith, I will live so long as I may, that's the certain
of it, and when I cannot live any longer, I will do as I
15   may. That is my rest, that is the rendezvous of it.

Bardolph   It is certain, corporal, that he is married to Nell
Quickly, and certainly she did you wrong, for you were
troth-plighted to her.

Nym   I cannot tell. Things must be as they may. Men
20   may sleep, and they may have their throats about them
at that time, and some say knives have edges. It must be
as it may. Though Patience be a tired mare, yet she will
plod. There must be conclusions. Well, I cannot tell.

[*Enter* **Pistol** *and* **Hostess**]

Bardolph   [*To* **Nym**] Here comes Ancient Pistol and his
25   wife. Good Corporal, be patient here.

Nym   How now, mine host Pistol!

Pistol   Base tick, call'st thou me host?
Now by this hand I swear I scorn the term.
Nor shall my Nell keep lodgers.

30 **Hostess**   No, by my troth, not long, for we cannot lodge
and board a dozen or fourteen gentlewomen that live
honestly by the prick of their needles, but it will be
thought we keep a bawdy-house straight.

[**Nym** *draws his sword*]

Bardolph   I'll treat you to a breakfast to make you
friends again, and we'll all go to France as three
sworn brothers. Say yes, good Corporal Nym.

Nym   'Strewth, I'll live as long as maybe, that's for
sure. When I can't live any longer, I'll do as maybe.
That's my lot. That's the termination of it.

Bardolph   He's married to Nell Quickly for sure,
corporal; and she certainly double-crossed you 'cos
you were engaged to her.

Nym   It's not for me to say. What will be, will be. Men
sleep . . . they may have their throats with them
when they do . . . and some say knives have sharp
edges . . . It's all as maybe. We must plod on. It will
all come right in the end. I say no more.

[*Enter* **Ensign Pistol**, *who speaks in an exaggerated
histrionic manner, and his wife* **Hostess Quickly**,
keeper of the Boar's Head Tavern]

Bardolph   'Morning, Ensign Pistol. [*To* **Nym**] Here
comes Ensign Pistol and his wife. Quietly now,
Corporal.

Nym   [*provocatively*] How's things, Landlord Pistol?

Pistol   [**Nym***'s superior in army rank*] You lousy
insect! Call you me a landlord? By God, I swear I
scorn the term! My Nell will take no lodgers!

Hostess   No, indeed, not for long, 'cos we can't board
and lodge a dozen or fourteen nice young ladies
who earn an honest living pricking away with their
needles, without people think we're running a
brothel!

[**Nym** *draws his sword*]

35   Oh well-a-day, Lady! If he be not hewn now, we shall
      see wilful adultery and murder committed.

      [**Pistol** *draws his sword*]

Bardolph   Good Lieutenant! Good Corporal! Offer nothing
      here.

Nym   Pish!

Pistol   Pish for thee, Iceland dog! Thou prick-eared cur of
40   Iceland!

Hostess   Good Corporal Nym, show thy valour, and put
      up your sword.

Nym   Will you shog off? I would have you solus.

Pistol   'Solus', egregious dog? Oh viper vile!
45   The 'solus' in thy most marvellous face,
      The 'solus' in thy teeth, and in thy throat,
      And in thy hateful lungs, yea in thy maw, perdy,
      And which is worse, within thy nasty mouth!
      I do retort the 'solus' in thy bowels.
50   For I can take, and Pistol's cock is up,
      And flashing fire will follow.

Nym   I am not Barbason, you cannot conjure me. I have
      an humour to knock you indifferently well. If you grow
      foul with me, Pistol, I will scour you with my rapier, as I
55   may, in fair terms. If you would walk off, I would prick
      your guts a little, in good terms, as I may, and that's the
      humour of it.

Pistol   Oh braggart vile, and damned furious wight!
      The grave doth gape and doting death is near.
60   Therefore exhale.

      [*He draws his sword*]

Oh, dear! Bless us, if he's not stopped short now, we'll see wilful adultery and murder committed!

[**Pistol** *draws his sword too*]

Bardolph   Lieutenant – Corporal – let's have no fighting!

Nym   [*making a rude gesture*] Pish!

Pistol   [*returning it*] And pish to you, you shaggy mongrel with the pointy ears!

Hostess   Good Corporal Nym, show how brave you are and put your sword away.

Nym   Get lost, will you? [*to* **Pistol**] I want you solo.

Pistol   Solo, you lousy dog? Oh, you filthy snake! Solo [*making a rude sign*] to your most marvellous face! Solo in your teeth; and in your throat; and in your hateful lungs! Yes, and in your guts, by God! And, what is worse, inside your loathsome mouth! Solo to your bowels! When Pistol's cocked he can destroy; a flash of firing follows!

Nym   I'm no devil! You can't get rid of me with words! I have a rum desire to give you a good hiding. Muck about with me Pistol, and I'll clean you out with my rapier, as maybe, no messing! Walk to one side and I'll prick your guts a little, no sweat, as maybe, and that's the rumness of it.

Pistol   [*dramatically*] Oh, loud mouth vile! Oh, damned mad-headed blighter! The grave opens wide and doting death is near! Therefore, extract!

[**Nym** *and* **Pistol** *draw their swords simultaneously*]

Bardolph   Hear me, hear me what I say.

[*He draws his sword*]

He that strikes the first stroke, I'll run him up to the
hilts, as I am a soldier.

Pistol   An oath of mickle might, and fury shall abate.

[*They sheathe their swords*]

65   [*To* **Nym**] Give me thy fist, thy forefoot to me give;
Thy spirits are most tall.

Nym   I will cut thy throat one time or other, in fair terms,
that is the humour of it.

Pistol   'Couple a gorge!'
70   That is the word. I thee defy again.
Oh hound of Crete, think'st thou my spouse to get?
No! To the spital go,
And from the powd'ring tub of infamy
Fetch forth the lazar kite of Cressid's kind,
75   Doll Tearsheet she by name, and her espouse.
I have, and I will hold, the quondam Quickly
For the only she, and – pauca, there's enough.
Go to.

[*Enter the* **Boy**]

Boy   Mine host Pistol, you must come to my master, and
80   you, hostess. He is very sick, and would to bed. Good
Bardolph, put thy nose between his sheets, and do the
office of a warming-pan. Faith, he's very ill.

Bardolph   Away, you rogue!

Bardolph   Listen! Listen to what I'm saying! [*He draws his sword too*] Whoever strikes first, I'll run him through right up to my hilt, as I'm a soldier!

Pistol   [*glad to avoid danger*] An oath of considerable potency, and anger shall subside . . .

[**Nym** *and* **Pistol** *replace their swords. To* **Nym**] Give me your hand. Your forepaw to me give! In spirit, you walk tall!

Nym   [*rejecting the peace offering*] I'll cut your throat some day, no messing, and that's the rumness of it!

Pistol   Cut throats? So that's the game? I defy you once again! [*He gestures rudely to stress his point*] Oh, lying hound! You hope my wife to win? No! It's the hospital for you, and from the V.D. ward, fetch forth the poxy whore with Cressida's complaint – Doll Tearsheet is her name. Take her to wife! I have, and I will keep, the former Mistress Quickly. The one and only, so nuff said. Get lost!

[*Enter a* **Boy**, *servant of* **Sir John Falstaff**, *a bosom friend of* **King Henry's** *in earlier days, and a notorious fat rogue when in his prime*]

Boy   Landlord Pistol, you must come to my master, and you too, Hostess. He's very sick, and has taken to his bed. Bardolph, put your nose between his sheets and warm him up! Honestly, he's very ill.

Bardolph   [*taking a swipe at him for his cheek*] Get away, you rogue!

Hostess   By my troth, he'll yield the crow a pudding one
85   of these days. The King has killed his heart. Good
husband, come home presently.

[*Exit* **Hostess** *and* **Boy**]

Bardolph   Come, shall I make you two friends? We must
to France together. Why the devil should we keep knives
to cut one another's throats?

90 **Pistol**   Let floods o'erswell, and fiends for food howl on!

Nym   You'll pay me the eight shillings I won of you at
betting?

Pistol   Base is the slave that pays.

Nym   That now I will have. That's the humour of it.

95 **Pistol**   As manhood shall compound. Push home.

[*They draw their swords*]

Bardolph   [*drawing his sword*] By this sword, he that makes
the first thrust, I'll kill him. By this sword, I will.

Pistol   Sword is an oath, and oaths must have their
course.

[*He sheathes his sword*]

100 **Bardolph**   Corporal Nym, an thou wilt be friends, be
friends. An thou wilt not, why then be enemies with me
too. Prithee, put up.

Nym   I shall have my eight shillings I won of you at
betting?

Hostess   [*supporting her husband*] He'll end up on
the gallows one of these days, I swear it. [*Sadly,
recalling that* **King Henry** *renounced* **Falstaff** *on
succeeding to the throne*] The King has broken his
heart. Good husband, go home right away.

[*She leaves, led by the* **Boy**]

Bardolph   Come now. Shall I make you two friends?
We must all go to France together. Why the devil
should we carry knives to cut each other's throats?

Pistol   Let oceans flood, and devils howl for food!

Nym   You'll pay me the forty pence I won from you at
betting?

Pistol   Cowardly is the wretch who pays his debts!

Nym   I'll have it now. That's the rumness of it.

Pistol   It shall be settled, then, the manly way. Have
at you!

[*They draw their swords again*]

Bardolph   [*drawing his*] By this sword, I'll kill the one
who makes the first thrust! By this sword, I will!

Pistol   [*once more saved from a showdown;
sheathing his sword*] 'Sword [*meaning God's word*]
is an oath. Oaths must be respected.

Bardolph   Corporal Nym, if you'll be friends, be
friends. If you won't, why then be enemies with me,
too! Come now: put that away!

Nym   Shall I get the forty pence I won from you at
gambling?

105 **Pistol**   A noble shalt thou have, and present pay,
       And liquor likewise will I give to thee;
       And friendship shall combine, and brotherhood.
       I'll live by Nym, and Nym shall live by me.
       Is not this just? For I shall sutler be
110   Unto the camp, and profits will accrue.
       Give me thy hand.

   Nym   I shall have my noble?

   Pistol   In cash, most justly paid.

   Nym   Well, then that's the humour of't.

   [**Nym** *and* **Bardolph** *sheathe their swords*]

   [*Enter* **Hostess**]

115 **Hostess**   As ever you come of women, come in quickly to
       Sir John. Ah, poor heart, he is so shaked of a burning
       quotidian tertian, that it is most lamentable to behold.
       Sweet men, come to him.

                                                          [*Exit*

   Nym   The King hath run bad humours on the knight,
120   that's the even of it.

   Pistol   Nym, thou hast spoke the right. His heart is
       fracted and corroborate.

   Nym   The King is a good king, but it must be as it may.
       He passes some humours and careers.

125 **Pistol**   Let us condole the knight; for, lambkins, we will
       live.

                                                          [*Exeunt*]

Pistol I'll give you thirty pence cash down. And liquor I will likewise give to you; and friendship too, and brotherhood. I'll live for Nym, and Nym shall live for me. Is not that fair? I'll be camp caterer, and profits will amass. Give me your hand!

Nym Shall I get my thirty pence?

Pistol In cash, as you deserve.

Nym Well then. That's the rumness of it. [*He sheathes his sword*]

[**Hostess Quickly** *enters*]

Hostess As ever you are mothers' sons, come quickly to Sir John! Ah, poor soul, he's got such bad pneumonica, it's really sad to see. Do come to him, dear gentlemen.

[*She dashes out again*]

Nym The King has done some rum things to the knight. That's the long and short of it.

Pistol Nym, you've never said a truer word. His heart is fractured and cumknockerated.

Nym The King is a good king. But it must be as maybe. He has some rummy ways.

Pistol Let us convey our sympathies to the knight. We're all right, my little lambs!

[*They go*]

Scene 2

Southampton. Enter the **Dukes of Exeter, Bedford** *and* **Westmorland.**

Bedford   'Fore God, his grace is bold, to trust these
    traitors.

Exeter   They shall be apprehended by and by.

Westmorland   How smooth and even they do bear
5   themselves,
    As if allegiance in their bosoms sat,
    Crowned with faith and constant loyalty!

Bedford   The King hath note of all that they intend,
    By interception which they dream not of.

10 **Exeter**   Nay, but the man that was his bedfellow,
    Whom he hath dulled and cloyed with gracious favours –
    That he should for a foreign purse so sell
    His sovereign's life to death and treachery!

Westmorland   Oh, the Lord Masham.

[*Sound trumpets. Enter the* **King, Scroop, Cambridge, Grey**
    and **Attendants**]

15 **King Henry**   Now sits the wind fair, and we will aboard.
    My lord of Cambridge, and my kind lord of Masham,
    And you, my gentle knight, give me your thoughts.
    Think you not that the powers we bear with us
    Will cut their passage through the force of France,
20   Doing the execution and the act
    For which we have in head assembled them?

Scroop   No doubt, my liege, if each man do his best.

Scene 2

The port of Southampton. Enter the **Dukes of Exeter** *and* **Bedford**, *and the* **Earl of Westmorland.**

Bedford   By God, His Grace is risking things to trust these traitors!

Exeter   They will be arrested by and by.

Westmorland   How cool and calm they are as if duty, faith and unwavering loyalty sat enthroned in their hearts!

Bedford   The King knows of all their plans by means of secret intelligence, which they don't dream exists.

Exeter   Yes: but the man who used to share a bed with him, on whom he has showered gracious favours – to think that he should sell his sovereign's life to death and treachery for a foreign bribe!

Westmorland   You mean Lord Masham?

[*Trumpets herald the entrance of* **King Henry, Lord Scroop, The Earl of Cambridge, Sir Thomas Grey,** *and* **Attendants**]

King Henry   The wind is in the right direction, and we will go on board. Lord Cambridge, and my kind Lord Masham, and you, Sir Thomas, give me your opinion. Do you agree that our forces will cut their way through those of France, carrying out the plan of campaign for which we conscripted them?

Scroop   Without a doubt, my liege, if each man does his best.

King Henry   I doubt not that, since we are well
   persuaded.
25   We carry not a heart with us from hence
   That grows not in a fair consent with ours,
   Nor leave not one behind that doth not wish
   Success and conquest to attend on us.

Cambridge   Never was monarch better feared and loved
30   Than is your majesty. There's not, I think, a subject
   That sits in heart-grief and uneasiness
   Under the sweet shade of your government.

Grey   True. Those that were your father's enemies
   Have steeped their galls in honey, and do serve you
35   With hearts create of duty and of zeal.

King Henry   We therefore have great cause of
   thankfulness,
   And shall forget the office of our hand
   Sooner than quittance of desert and merit,
40   According to their weight and worthiness.

Scroop   So service shall with steeled sinews toil,
   And labour shall refresh itself with hope,
   To do your grace incessant services.

King Henry   We judge no less. Uncle of Exeter,
45   Enlarge the man committed yesterday
   That railed against our person. We consider
   It was excess of wine that set him on,
   And on his more advice we pardon him.

Scroop   That's mercy, but too much security.
50   Let him be punished, sovereign, lest example
   Breed, by his sufferance, more of such a kind.

King Henry   Oh let us yet be merciful.

Cambridge   So may your highness, and yet punish too.

King Henry   I don't doubt that, since we are confident there's not a man in the expedition whose heart is not at one with ours; nor do we leave a single one behind who doesn't wish success and victory on us.

Cambridge   Never was a monarch more respected and loved than is Your Majesty. There's not, I think, one subject who sits dissatisfied or discontented under the benign protection of your government.

Grey   True. Your father's old enemies have changed from sour to sweet, and now serve you with hearts composed of duty and of zeal.

King Henry   We therefore have much to be thankful for, and would lose a hand sooner than neglect reward for worthiness and merit.

Scroop   So, toil on your behalf shall be unstinted – the tasks made lighter by hopeful prospects – in order to give Your Grace unceasing service.

King Henry   We would expect nothing less. Uncle Exeter, set free the man imprisoned yesterday who spoke insultingly against us. We think he'd had too much to drink. Now he's thought better of it, we pardon him.

Scroop   That's merciful, but too imprudent. He should be punished, sovereign, in case his being pardoned breeds others of the same kind.

King Henry   Oh, let's be merciful for once.

Cambridge   So Your Highness can be, and yet still punish him.

Grey Sir, you show great mercy if you give him life,
55 After the taste of much correction.

King Henry Alas, your too much love and care of me
Are heavy orisons 'gainst this poor wretch!
If little faults proceeding on distemper
Shall not be winked at, how shall we stretch our eye
60 When capital crimes, chewed, swallowed, and digested,
Appear before us? We'll yet enlarge that man,
Though Cambridge, Scroop, and Grey, in their dear care
And tender preservation of our person,
Would have him punished. And now to our French
65   causes.
Who are the late commissioners?

Cambridge   I one, my lord
Your highness bade me ask for it today.

Scroop So did you me, my liege.

70 **Grey**   And I, my royal sovereign

King Henry Then Richard, Earl of Cambridge, there is
yours;
There yours, Lord Scroop of Masham, and Sir Knight,
Grey of Northumberland, this same is yours.
75 Read them, and know I know your worthiness.
My lord of Westmorland, and Uncle Exeter,
We will aboard tonight. Why, how now, gentlemen?
What see you in those papers, that you lose
So much complexion? Look ye how they change:
80 Their cheeks are paper. Why, what read you there
That have so cowarded and chased your blood
Out of appearance?

Grey   Sir, you would be showing great mercy if you granted him his life after experiencing severe punishment.

King Henry   Alas, your excessive love and concern for me are strong pleas against this poor wretch. If small faults caused by drunkenness shall not be winked at, how shall we look upon capital crimes — detected, investigated and proven — when they appear before us? We'll still free that man, though Cambridge, Scroop and Grey, in their deep concern for the care and protection of our person, would have him punished. And now to our French affairs. Who were appointed recently to deputise for me in my absence?

Cambridge   I was one, my lord. Your Highness instructed me to ask for my commission today.

Scroop   Likewise me, my liege.

Grey   And I, my royal sovereign.

King Henry   [*handing out documents*] Then, Richard Earl of Cambridge, there is yours. There yours, Lord Scroop of Masham; and Sir Thomas Grey of Northumberland — this one is yours. Read them, and you will know I am aware of how worthy you are. [*Turning aside*] My Lord of Westmorland and Uncle Exeter, we'll embark tonight. [*Turning back to the rebels in mock surprise*] Why, what's the matter, gentlemen? What have you seen in those documents that make you turn so pale? Look how they've changed colour: their cheeks are as white as paper! Why, what have you read there to have caused the blood to drain from your faces?

Cambridge   I do confess my faul
    And do submit me to your highness' mercy.

85 **Grey, Scroop**   To which we all appeal.

  King Henry   The mercy that was quick in us but late
    By your own counsel is suppressed and killed.
    You must not dare, for shame, to talk of mercy,
    For your own reasons turn into your bosoms,
90   As dogs upon their masters, worrying you.
    See you, my princes and my noble peers,
    These English monsters? My lord of Cambridge here,
    You know how apt our love was to accord
    To furnish him with all appurtenants
95   Belonging to his honour; and this vile man
    Hath for a few light crowns lightly conspired
    And sworn unto the practices of France
    To kill us here in Hampton. To the which
    This knight, no less for bounty bound to us
100 Than Cambridge is, hath likewise sworn. But oh,
    What shall I say to thee, Lord Scroop, thou cruel,
    Ingrateful, savage, and inhuman creature?
    Thou that didst bear the key of all my counsels,
    That knew'st the very bottom of my soul,
105 That almost mightst have coined me into gold
    Wouldst thou have practised on me for thy use:
    May it be possible that foreign hire
    Could out of thee extract one spark of evil
    That might annoy my finger? 'Tis so strange
110 That though the truth of it stands off as gross
    As black and white, my eye will scarcely see it.
    Treason and murder ever kept together,
    As two yoke-devils sworn to either's purpose,
    Working so grossly in a natural cause
115 That admiration did not whoop at them;
    But thou, 'gainst all proportion, didst bring in

Cambridge   [*falling to his knees*] I confess to my offence, and throw myself upon Your Highness's mercy.

Grey, Scroop   To which we all appeal.

King Henry   The mercy that was active in us so recently is, by your own advice, supressed and killed. You must not dare, for shame, to talk of mercy; your own arguments turn against you, like dogs upon their masters, to your detriment. [*Turning to the court*] Do you see these English monsters? My Lord of Cambridge here: you know how readily we provided him with the wherewithal appropriate to his rank. Yet this vile man has, for a few wretched gold coins, wretchedly conspired and pledged himself to participate in the plots with France, to kill us here in Southampton. To which end this knight [*indicating* **Sir Thomas Grey**] – no less obliged to us for our generosity than Cambridge is – has similarly sworn an oath. But oh, what shall I say to you, Lord Scroop, you cruel, ungrateful, savage and inhuman creature? You, privy to all my secrets; who knew me intimately; who almost could have turned me into gold, if you'd resolved to do so, for your own purposes: can it be possible that a foreign bribe could tempt one spark of evil out of you that could harm so much as my finger? It's so amazing that though it stands out as plain as black and white, I can hardly believe it. Treason and murder always go hand-in-hand: like two interlinked evils dedicated to acting in concert; working together so naturally in wickedness that nobody finds it surprising. But – against all human decency – you introduced novelty

Wonder to wait on treason and on murder.
And whatsoever cunning fiend it was
That wrought upon thee so preposterously
120 Hath got the voice in hell for excellence.
And other devils that suggest by treasons
Do botch and bungle up damnation
With patches, colours, and with forms, being fetched
From glist'ring semblances of piety;
125 But he that tempered thee, bade thee stand up,
Gave thee no instance why thou shouldst do treason,
Unless to dub thee with the name of traitor.
If that same demon that hath gulled thee thus
Should with his lion gait walk the whole world,
130 He might return to vasty Tartar back
And tell the legions, 'I can never win
A soul as easy as that Englishman's.'
Oh how hast thou with jealousy infected
The sweetness of affiance! Show men dutiful?
135 Why so didst thou. Seem they grave and learned?
Why so didst thou. Come they of noble family?
Why so didst thou. Seem they religious?
Why so didst thou. Or are they spare in diet,
Free from gross passion, or of mirth or anger,
140 Constant in spirit, not swerving with the blood,
Garnished and decked in modest complement,
Not working with the eye without the ear,
And but in purged judgement trusting neither?
Such, and so finely bolted, didst thou seem.
145 And thus thy fall hath left a kind of blot
To mark the full-fraught man, and best indued,
With some suspicion. I will weep for thee,
For this revolt of thine, methinks, is like
Another fall of man. Their faults are open.
150 Arrest them to the answer of the law,
And God acquit them of their practices!

into the service of treason and murder. Whoever the
cunning fiend was who corrupted you, he must be
voted best in hell for excellence! All the other devils
who tempt by means of treason make their fiendish
work seem virtuous, with cosmetic touches,
plausible pretexts, and false conduct – all derived
from superficial illusions of virtuousness. But the
one who tempted you, who made you rebel, offered
no motive for committing treason, unless it was to
knight you as 'Sir Traitor'. If the very devil who
tricked you like that should roam the whole world
like the proverbial roaring lion, he could return to
hideous hell and tell the fallen angels 'I can never
win a soul so easy as I did that Englishman's'. Oh,
how you have tainted the sweetness of trust with
suspicion! Do men act dutifully? Why, so did you.
Do they seem grave and learned? Why, so did you.
Do they come from noble families? Why, so did
you. Do they seem religious? Why, so did you. Or
are they abstemious with their food; free from
excessive emotions, either of mirth or anger; stable
in temperament, not moved by passion; outwardly
conservative in appearance and behaviour; not
merely using their eyes, but listening also with their
ears – and trusting neither without confirmation?
Such, and so ultra-perfect, did you seem. So your
fall has left a kind of blot to stain with some
suspicion the man of sterling qualities. I will weep
for you, because this revolt of yours is like another
fall of man. [*To* **Exeter**] Their crimes are obvious.
Arrest them in the name of the law, and God
forgive them for their misdeeds.

Exeter   I arrest thee of high treason, by the name of
Richard, Earl of Cambridge. I arrest thee of high
treason, by the name of Henry, Lord Scroop of
155   Masham. I arrest thee of high treason, by the name of
Thomas Grey, knight, of Northumberland.

Scroop   Our purposes God justly hath discovered,
And I repent my fault more than my death,
Which I beseech your highness to forgive
160   Although my body pay the price of it.

Cambridge   For me, the gold of France did not seduce,
Although I did admit it as a motive
The sooner to effect what I intended.
But God be thanked for prevention,
165   Which I in sufferance heartily will rejoice,
Beseeching God and you to pardon me.

Grey   Never did faithful subject more rejoice
At the discovery of most dangerous treason
Than I do at this hour joy o'er myself,
170   Prevented from a damned enterprise.
My fault, but not my body, pardon, sovereign.

King Henry   God quit you in his mercy. Hear your
sentence.
You have conspired against our royal person,
175   Joined with an enemy proclaimed,
And from his coffers
Received the golden earnest of our death,
Wherein you would have sold your king to slaughter,
His princes and his peers to servitude,
180   His subjects to oppression and contempt,
And his whole kingdom into desolation.
Touching our person seek we no revenge,
But we our kingdom's safety must so tender,
Whose ruin you have sought, that to her laws

Exeter   I arrest you for high treason, Richard, Earl of Cambridge. I arrest you for high treason, Henry, Lord Scroop of Masham. I arrest you for high treason Thomas Grey, Knight, of Northumberland.

[**Attendants** *seize the three conspirators*]

Scroop   God has rightly exposed our plot, and I regret my fault more than I do my death. I beseech Your Highness to forgive it, although I must pay the price with my body.

Cambridge   In my case, it was not French gold that tempted me, though I admit it was a means of achieving my objectives all the sooner. But God be thanked for preventing us. I heartily rejoice at it, though suffering the penalty; beseeching God and you to pardon me.

Grey   Never did a faithful subject rejoice more at the exposure of perilous treason than I, at this present moment, rejoice over myself: thwarted in an evil enterprise. Pardon my fault, but not my body, sovereign.

King Henry   God forgive you in his mercy. Hear your sentence. You have conspired against our royal person, joined with a declared enemy, and from his treasury received advance payment for our death: thereby selling your king to slaughter, his princes and nobility to slavery, his subjects to oppression and abuse, and his whole kingdom into desolation. Personally, we seek no revenge; but we must be so mindful of the safety of our kingdom – whose ruin you have sought – that we deliver you to her laws.

185   We do deliver you. Get you therefore hence,
       Poor miserable wretches, to your death;
       The taste whereof, God of his mercy give
       You patience to endure, and true repentance
       Of all your dear offences. Bear them hence.

                              [*Exeunt the traitors, guarded*

190   Now lords for France, the enterprise whereof
       Shall be to you, as us, like glorious.
       We doubt not of a fair and lucky war,
       Since God so graciously hath brought to light
       This dangerous treason lurking in our way
195   To hinder our beginnings. We doubt not now
       But every rub is smoothed on our way.
       Then forth, dear countrymen. Let us deliver
       Our puissance into the hand of God,
       Putting it straight in expedition.
200   Cheerly to sea; the signs of war advance;
       No king of England, if not king of France!

                              [*Flourish of trumpets. Exeunt*

Scene 3

Eastcheap. The Boar's Head Tavern. Enter **Pistol, Nym, Bardolph, Boy** *and* **Hostess.**

Hostess   Prithee, honey sweet husband, let me bring thee
to Staines.

Pistol   No, for my manly heart doth yearn.
       Bardolph, be blithe; Nym, rouse thy vaunting veins;
5   Boy, bristle thy courage up; for Falstaff he is dead,
       And we must earn therefore.

Go then from here, poor miserable wretches, to
your deaths; and may God give you patience to
endure them and true repentance of all your dire
offences. Take them away.

[*The traitors are led away under guard*]

Now, lords, to France! Which enterprise shall be to
you, and to us, equally glorious. We have no doubt
that the war will be a good and lucky one, since
God has so graciously brought to light this
dangerous treason that lurked in our way and
hindered us at the start. We have no doubt that all
obstacles have now been overcome. So let us go,
dear countrymen. Let us deliver our army into the
hand of God, and start immediately. Off to sea!
Raise the flags of war! Never a King of England if
not King of France!

[*They go*]

Scene 3

Enter **Ensign Pistol, Corporal Nym, Lieutenant
Bardolph, Boy** *and* **Hostess Quickly.**

Hostess   Please, dear sweet husband, let me stay with
you as far as Staines.

Pistol   No; my manly heart is struck with grief.
Bardolph, cheer up! Nym, put colour in your
cheeks! Boy, brush up your courage! Falstaff is
dead. Therefore we must work.

Hostess   A did in some sort, indeed, handle women – but
35   then he was rheumatic, and talked of the Whore of
Babylon.

Boy   Do you not remember, a saw a flea stick upon
Bardolph's nose, and a said it was a black soul burning
in hell.

40 **Bardolph**   Well, the fuel is gone that maintained that fire.
That's all the riches I got in his service.

Nym   Shall we shog? The King will be gone from
Southampton.

Pistol   Come, let's away. My love, give me thy lips.
45   Look to my chattels and my movables.
Let senses rule. The word is 'Pitch and pay'.
Trust none, for oaths are straws, men's faiths are wafer-
cakes,
And Holdfast is the only dog, my duck.
50   Therefore Caveto be thy counsellor.
Go, clear thy crystals. Yokefellows in arms,
Let us to France, like horse-leeches, my boys,
To suck, to suck, the very blood to suck!

Boy   And that's but unwholesome food, they say.

55 **Pistol**   Touch her soft mouth, and march.

Bardolph   Farewell, hostess.

[*He kisses her*]

Nym   I cannot kiss, that is the humour of it, but adieu.

Pistol   [*to* **Hostess**] Let housewifery appear. Keep close, I
thee command.

60 **Hostess**   Fairwell! Adieu!

[*Exeunt*]

Hostess   He did indeed, in a sort of way, discuss women, but then he was a bit delirious, and talked about the Whore of Babylon.

Boy   Do you remember when he saw a flea stuck to Bardolph's nose, and said it was a black soul burning in hell?

Bardolph   Well, the fuel has gone that kept that fire going. [*Pointing to his nose*] That's the only riches I ever got from working for him.

Nym   Shall we go? The King will have left Southampton.

Pistol   Come, we must be off. [*To* **Hostess Quickly**] My love, give me a kiss! Guard my goods and chattels. Let common sense prevail. The rule is 'cash, no credit'. Trust none, for promises are vain. Men's vows are wafer thin. Hold fast to what is yours, my duck! Let caution be your guide. Go, dry your eyes. Comrades in arms, let's go to France like horse-leeches, my boys! To suck . . . to suck . . . to suck them absolutely dry!

Boy   [*aside*] And that's not good for you, they say . . .

Pistol   Touch her soft lips, and go!

Bardolph   Farewell, hostess! [*He kisses her*]

Nym   I can't kiss, that's the rumness of it. But – goodbye.

Pistol   [*to* **Hostess**] Think twice before you spend. My orders are: be frugal!

Hostess   Farewell! Adieu!

[*They go their separate ways*]

85

Scene 4

France; the King's palace. Flourish. Enter the **French King,**
the **Dauphin,** *and the* **Duke of Britaine, Constable** *and*
others.

French King   Thus comes the English with full power
    upon us,
    And more than carefully it us concerns
    To answer royally in our defences.
5   Therefore the Dukes of Berri and of Britaine,
    Of Brabant and of Orleans shall make forth,
    And you, Prince Dauphin, with all swift dispatch
    To line and new repair our towns of war
    With men of courage and with means defendant.
10   For England his approaches makes as fierce
    As waters to the sucking of a gulf.
    It fits us then to be as provident
    As fear may teach us, out of late examples
    Left by the fatal and neglected English
15   Upon our fields.

Dauphin   My most redoubted father
    It is most meet we arm us 'gainst the foe;
    For peace itself should not so dull a kingdom,
    Though war, nor no known quarrel, were in question,
20   But that defences, musters, preparations
    Should be maintained, assembled, and collected
    As were a war in expectation.
    Therefore, I say, 'tis meet we all go forth
    To view the sick and feeble parts of France.
25   And let us do it with no show of fear –
    No, with no more than if we heard that England
    Were busied with a Whitsun morris dance.

Scene 4

France: the King's palace. A flourish of trumpets preceeds the entry of **King Charles VI of France**, *the* **Dauphin, The Constable**, *and the* **Dukes of Berri** *and* **Britaine**.

King Charles   The English are advancing towards us at full strength, and to respond royally in our own defence is our major concern. Therefore the Dukes of Berri, Britaine, Brabant and Orleans, together with you, Prince Dauphin, will go at once to reinforce and renovate our front-line towns, with men of courage and defensive equipment. As for the King of England, his advance thrust is as fierce as the currents round a whirlpool. Our recent experiences of defeat by the deadly and underestimated English should teach us to be cautious.

Dauphin   My most respected father. It's quite right that we should arm ourselves against the enemy. Even when there's neither threat of war nor any known reason for one, peace should not make a kingdom so complacent that defences, troops and preparations are not maintained, mustered and organised as if one were expected. Therefore, I say, it's right that we should inspect the vulnerable regions of France. And let us do so without appearing afraid; no, no more than if we heard that England was busy preparing a Whitsun morris

For, my good liege, she is so idly kinged,
Her sceptre so fantastically borne
30   By a vain, giddy, shallow, humorous youth,
That fear attends her not.

Constable   Oh peace, Prince Dauphin
You are too much mistaken in this king.
Question your grace the late ambassadors
35   With what regard he heard their embassy,
How well supplied with aged counsellors,
How modest in exception, and withal
How terrible in constant resolution,
And you shall find his vanities forespent
40   Were but the outside of the Roman Brutus,
Covering discretion with a coat of folly,
As gardeners do with ordure hide those roots
That shall first spring and be most delicate.

Dauphin   Well, 'tis not so, my Lord High Constable.
45   But though we think it so, it is no matter.
In cases of defence 'tis best to weigh
The enemy more mighty than he seems.
So the proportions of defence are filled;
Which, of a weak and niggardly projection,
50   Doth like a miser spoil his coat with scanting
A little cloth.

French King   Think we King Harry strong;
And princes, look you strongly arm to meet him.
The kindred of him hath been fleshed upon us,
55   And he is bred out of that bloody strain
That haunted us in our familiar paths.
Witness our too much memorable shame
When Crecy battle fatally was struck,
And all our princes captived by the hand
60   Of that black name, Edward, Black Prince of Wales;

dance. Because, my good liege, she has so frivolous
a king, her royal office is so zanily filled by a vain,
silly, shallow, wayward youth that she offers no
threat.

Constable   One moment, Prince Dauphin. You've got
this king all wrong. Your Grace should ask the
recent ambassadors how impressively he received
their message, how well supplied he is with elder
statesmen, how restrained he was in his reactions,
while at the same time being so formidable in his
fixed determination. Then you'll discover that his
youthful follies were like the outward behaviour of
the Roman Brutus, who hid his intelligence beneath
a cloak of insanity – just as gardeners cover the
roots of early, exquisite flowers with manure.

Dauphin   Well, that's not so, my Lord High Constable.
But what we think is irrelevant. In cases of defence,
it's best to regard the enemy as more powerful than
he seems, to ensure that the scale of defence is
correct. If it's underestimated, it's akin to a miser
spoiling a coat for want of a little more cloth.

King Charles   We'll assume King Harry is strong.
Therefore, princes, be sure you arm yourselves
strongly to confront him. His fellow countrymen
have had their first taste of blood; and he is of the
warlike breed that came hunting us on our home
ground. Witness our never-to-be-forgotten shame
when we clashed at the battle of Crecy, and all our
princes were taken captive by Edward, the rightly-
named Black Prince of Wales. His eminent father,

Whiles that his mountain sire, on mountain standing,
Up in the air, crowned with the golden sun,
Saw his heroical seed and smiled to see him
Mangle the work of nature and deface
65   The patterns that by God and by French fathers
Had twenty years been made. This is a stem
Of that victorious stock, and let us fear
The native mightiness and fate of him.

[*Enter a* **Messenger**]

Messenger   Ambassadors from Harry, King of England,
70   Do crave admittance to your majesty.

French King   We'll give them present audience. Go and
bring them.

[*Exit* **Messenger**

You see this chase is hotly followed, friends.

Dauphin   Turn head and stop pursuit; for coward dogs
75   Most spend their mouths when what they seem to
threaten
Runs far before them. Good my sovereign,
Take up the English short, and let them know
Of what a monarchy you are the head.
80   Self-love, my liege, is not so vile a sin
As self-neglecting.

[*Enter* **Exeter,** *and Train*]

French King   From our brother England:

Exeter   From him, and thus he greets your majesty:
He wills you, in the name of God Almighty,
85   That you divest yourself and lay apart
The borrowed glories that by gift of heaven,
By law of nature and of nations, 'longs
To him and to his heirs: namely the crown,

90

from a mountain-top on high, crowned with the sun's golden rays, saw his heroic offspring and smiled to see him maul the God-given, twenty-year-old sons of French fathers. He descends from that victorious stock, so let us fear his inborn mightiness and destiny.

[*A* **Messenger** *enters*]

Messenger   Ambassadors from Harry, King of England, beg admission to your Majesty.

King Charles   We'll see them at once. Go and bring them.

[*The* **Messenger** *leaves*]

You see how close they are upon our heels, my friends.

Dauphin   Stand your ground and stop the hunt. Cowardly dogs bark loudest when their quarry is a long way off. Good my sovereign, call the English bluff, and let them know what kind of monarchy it is you head. Self-love is not so great a sin as self-abasement.

[*The* **Duke of Exeter** *enters*]

King Charles   From our brother England?

Exeter   From him, and he greets Your Majesty thus. In the name of God Almighty, he would have you renounce and set aside the borrowed titles and privileges that by God's gift, and human and divine right, belong to him and to his heirs: namely, the

And all wide-stretched honours that pertain
90   By custom and the ordinance of times
Unto the crown of France. That you may know
'Tis no sinister nor no awkward claim,
Picked from the worm-holes of long-vanished days,
Nor from the dust of old oblivion raked,
95   He sends you this most memorable line,
In every branch truly demonstrative,
Willing you overlook this pedigree,
And when you find him evenly derived
From his most famed of famous ancestors,
100   Edward the Third, he bids you then resign
Your crown and kingdom, indirectly held
From him, the native and true challenger.

French King   Or else what follows?

Exeter   Bloody constraint. For if you hide the crown
105   Even in your hearts, there will he rake for it.
Therefore in fierce tempest is he coming,
In thunder and in earthquake, like a Jove,
That if requiring fail, he will compel;
And bids you, in the bowels of the Lord,
110   Deliver up the crown, and to take mercy
On the poor souls for whom this hungry war
Opens his vasty jaws; and on your head
Turning the widows' tears, the orphans' cries,
The dead men's blood, the pining maidens' groans,
115   For husbands, fathers, and betrothed lovers
That shall be swallowed in this controversy.
This is his claim, his threat'ning, and my message –
Unless the Dauphin be in presence here,
To whom expressly I bring greeting too.

120 **French King**   For us, we will consider of this further.
Tomorrow shall you bear our full intent
Back to our brother of England.

crown, and all the wide-ranging honours that go with it, by custom and practice over the ages. To prove to you that it is no irregular or trumped-up claim – resurrected from antiquity, or raked up from the dust of the dim and distant past – he sends you this convincing family tree, every branch a confirmation. [*He gives* **King Charles** *a parchment roll*] He wishes you to look this pedigree over, and when you discover that he is directly descended from his most famed of famous ancestors – Edward the Third – he instructs you then to resign your crown and kingdom, improperly held from him, the legitimate and true claimant.

King Charles   Or else what will happen?

Exeter   War. For even if you hide the crown inside your hearts, he'll go searching for it. Therefore he is coming like a Jove, in fierce tempest, in thunder, and in earthquake. If asking fails, he will compel. He bids you, in the bowels of Christ, to deliver up the crown, and to have mercy on the poor souls whom this hungry war will greedily devour. He places the responsibility on your head for widows' tears, orphans' cries, dead men's blood, the groans of pining maidens, for husbands, fathers, and engaged lovers who will be swallowed up by this dispute. This is his claim, his warning, and my message – unless the Dauphin is present here, to whom I bring a personal greeting.

King Charles   As for us, we will give this further consideration. Tomorrow you can take our final decision back to our brother the King of England.

Dauphin   For the Dauphin
I stand here for him. What to him from England?

125 **Exeter**   Scorn and defiance, slight regard, contempt:
And anything that may not misbecome
The mighty sender, doth he prize you at.
Thus says my king: an if your father's highness
Do not, in grant of all demands at large,
130 Sweeten the bitter mock you sent his majesty,
He'll call you to so hot an answer for it
That caves and womby vaultages of France
Shall chide your trespass and return your mock
In second accent of his ordinance.

135 **Dauphin**   Say if my father render fair return,
It is against my will; for I desire
Nothing but odds with England. To that end,
As matching to his youth and vanity,
I did present him with the Paris balls.

140 **Exeter**   He'll make your Paris Louvre shake for it,
Were it the mistress-court of mighty Europe.
And be assured, you'll find a difference,
As we his subjects have in wonder found,
Between the promise of his greener days
145 And these he masters now. How he weighs time
Even to the utmost grain, that you shall read
In your own losses, if he stay in France.

French King   Tomorrow shall you know our mind at full.

[*Flourish*]

Exeter   Dispatch us with all speed, lest that our king
150 Come here himself to question our delay;
For he is footed in this land already.

Dauphin   As for the Dauphin, I stand here for him. What's England's message to him?

Exeter   Scorn and defiance, disdain, contempt! And he rates you at anything not beneath the mighty sender's dignity. That's what my King says, and if the King your father, by granting all demands in full, does not sweeten the bitter mock you sent his majesty, he'll take you to task so fiercely for it that France's caves and hollow caverns will curse your misdeed, and return your mockery by echoing the sound of his artillery.

Dauphin   If my father replies politely, it will be against my will; because I desire nothing but conflict with England. That was why, in keeping with his youth and folly, I gave him the tennis balls.

Exeter   He'll make your palace shake for that, even if it were the finest court in mighty Europe. And be assured: you'll be amazed, as we his subjects have been, at the difference between the expectations of his callow youth and his behaviour now. He takes life very seriously now; as you'll learn to your cost if he stays in France.

King Charles   You will have our decision tomorrow.

[*He rises to his feet. Trumpets sound*]

Exeter   See we return with all speed, in case our King comes here himself to question our delay; he has already landed in this country.

French King   You shall be soon dispatched with fair
conditions.

A night is but small breath and little pause

155   To answer matters of this consequence.

[Flourish. Exeun

King Charles   You shall soon be dispatched with a
   considered reply. A night is a small breathing space
   and little delay in answering matters of such
   consequence.

   [*Trumpets sound again as he leaves and the court
   follows*]

Act three

Enter **Chorus**

Chorus   Thus with imagined wing our swift scene flies
    In motion of no less celerity
    Than that of thought. Suppose that you have seen
    The well-appointed king at Dover pier
5   Embark his royalty, and his brave fleet
    With silken streamers the young Phoebus fanning.
    Play with your fancies, and in them behold
    Upon the hempen tackle ship-boys climbing;
    Hear the shrill whistle, which doth order give
10   To sounds confused; behold the threaden sails,
    Borne with th' invisible and creeping wind,
    Draw the huge bottoms through the furrowed sea,
    Breasting the lofty surge. Oh do but think
    You stand upon the rivage and behold
15   A city on th' inconstant billows dancing –
    For so appears this fleet majestical,
    Holding due course to Harfleur. Follow, follow!
    Grapple your minds to sternage of this navy,
    And leave your England, as dead midnight still,
20   Guarded with grandsires, babies, and old women,
    Either past or not arrived to pith and puissance.
    For who is he, whose chin is but enriched
    With one appearing hair, that will not follow
    These culled and choice-drawn cavaliers to France?
25   Work, work your thoughts, and therein see a siege.
    Behold the ordnance on their carriages,
    With fatal mouths gaping on girded Harfleur.

Act three

The **Announcer** *enters.*

Announcer   Thus, with imaginary wings, our scene
flies swiftly on, with no less speed than that of
thought. Pretend that you have seen the well-
equipped king at Dover pier embark with royal
pomp, his gallant fleet bedecked with silken
streamers in imitation of the rising sun. Let your
imaginations wander, and see young sailors
climbing up the ropes; hear the bosun's whistle
which brings order out of chaos; behold the woven
sails, driven by the invisible and stealthy wind, draw
the huge ships through the wavy sea, forging their
way forward through the lofty swell! Oh, just think
you are standing on the shore, and you can see a
city dancing on the surging billows – for that's what
this majestic fleet looks like as it makes directly for
Harfleur. Follow it, follow it! Let your minds be
towed behind this navy and leave your England
quiet as the midnight hour, guarded by
grandfathers, babies and old women, either past
their prime or not arrived at full maturity. Who, with
so little as one hair upon his chin, would not follow
these select and hand-picked gentlemen-at-arms to
France? Work, work on your thoughts, and imagine
a siege. Behold the cannon on the mountings, their
deadly barrels pointing at stricken Harfleur.

Suppose the ambassador from the French comes back,
Tells Harry that the King doth offer him
30   Katherine his daughter, and with her, to dowry,
Some petty and unprofitable dukedoms.
The offer likes not, and the nimble gunner
With linstock now the devilish cannon touches,

[*Alarum, and chambers go off*]

And down goes all before them. Still be kind,
35   And eke out our performance with your mind.

[*Exit*

Scene 1

France. Before Harfleur. Alarum. Enter the **King** *and the
English army, with scaling ladders.*

King Henry   Once more unto the breach, dear friends,
      once more,
   Or close the wall up with our English dead.
   In peace there's nothing so becomes a man
5   As modest stillness and humility;
   But when the blast of war blows in our ears,
   Then imitate the action of the tiger,
   Stiffen the sinews, summon up the blood,
   Disguise fair nature with hard-favoured rage.
10   Then lend the eye a terrible aspect,
   Let it pry through the portage of the head
   Like the brass cannon; let the brow o'erwhelm it
   As fearfully as doth a galled rock
   O'erhang and jutty his confounded base,
15   Swilled with the wild and wasteful ocean.

Suppose that the ambassador comes back from the French and tells Harry that the king offers him his daughter Katherine and with her, as her dowry, some insignificant and worthless dukedoms. The offer is rejected, and the dexterous gunner touches off the devilish cannon with his taper –

[*The sound of gunfire is heard*]

– and down goes all before them! Bear with us still, and fill out our performance with your thoughts . . .

[*He goes*]

Scene 1

Outside the besieged town of Harfleur. Noises of war are loud now. The walls of the town have been breached by artillery, and it is the task of soldiers to break through into the town. **King Henry** *enters, with troops carrying scaling ladders.*

King Henry   Once more: charge into the gap, dear friends! Once more – or block the wall up with our English dead! In peacetime, there's nothing so becomes a man as meekness and humility. But when we hear the call to arms, then act like tigers: brace the muscles, stir the blood, disguise your tender feelings behind a mask of grim-faced fury! Next, give your eyes a terrifying look: let them protrude like brass cannons out of portholes. Frown, with all the frightfulness of a sea-tormented cliff that overhangs its eroded base, washed by the wild

Now set the teeth and stretch the nostril wide,
Hold hard the breath, and bend up every spirit
To his full height. On, on, you noblest English,
Whose blood is fet from fathers of war-proof,
20   Fathers that like so many Alexanders
Have in these parts from morn till even fought.
And sheathed their swords for lack of argument.
Dishonour not your mothers; now attest
That those whom you called fathers did beget you.
25   Be copy now to men of grosser blood,
And teach them how to war. And you, good yeomen,
Whose limbs were made in England, show us here
The mettle of your pasture; let us swear
That you are worth your breeding – which I doubt not,
30   For there is none of you so mean and base
That hath not noble lustre in your eyes.
I see you stand like greyhounds in the slips,
Straining upon the start. The game's afoot.
Follow your spirit, and upon this charge
35   Cry 'God for Harry; England and Saint George!'

[*Alarum, and chambers go off. Exeunt*

Scene 2

Before Harfleur. Enter **Nym, Bardolph, Pistol** and **Boy.**

Bardolph   On, on, on, on, on! To the breach, to the
breach!

and destructive ocean. Now grit your teeth, and flare your nostrils wide; take a deep breath and strain every faculty to its uttermost. On, on you most noble English, whose blood derives from fathers proved in war: fathers who, like so many Alexander the Greats, have fought in these parts from dawn till dusk, and put their swords away for lack of opposition. Do not dishonour your mothers; prove now that those you called your fathers really did beget you. Be examples now to lesser men, and teach them how to fight a war. And you, good yeomen, of stout English stock, show us here what you are made of: let us certify that you have worthy pedigrees – of which I have no doubt, for not one of you is so humble or base-born that your eyes lack noble lustre.

I see you stand like greyhounds in their slip-leads, straining to start. The whistle's blown. Follow your instinct, and as we charge, shout 'God for Harry, England and St George!'

[*The noise of battle increases. Cannons fire. The* **King** *and his soldiers make for the breach*]

Scene 2

Near the breach. **Nym, Bardolph, Pistol** *and* **Boy** *enter.*

Bardolph   [*commanding from behind*] On, on, on, on, on! To the breach! To the breach!

Nym   Pray thee corporal, stay. The knocks are too hot,
and for mine own part I have not a case of lives. The
5   humour of it is too hot, and that is the very plainsong of
it.

Pistol   'The plainsong' is most just, for humours do
abound.
Knocks go and come, God's vassals drop and die,
10   *And sword and shield*
In bloody field
    Doth win immortal fame.

Boy   Would I were in an alehouse in London. I would give
all my fame for a pot of ale, and safety.

15 **Pistol**   And I.
    If wishes would prevail with me
    My purpose should not fail with me
        But thither would I hie.

Boy   *As duly*
20   *But not as truly*
        As bird doth sing on bough.

    [*Enter* **Fluellen**]

Fluellen   Up to the breach, you dogs! Avaunt, you
cullions!

Pistol   Be merciful, great duke, to men of mould.
25   Abate thy rage, abate thy manly rage,
    Abate thy rage, great duke. Good bawcock, bate
    Thy rage. Use lenity, sweet chuck.

Nym   These be good humours! – Your honour wins bad
humours.

[*Exeunt all but the* **Boy**]

Nym   [*coming to a sharp halt*] Hold it, Corporal, will you? The barrage is getting too hot, and speaking for myself, I haven't got nine lives. The rumness of it is too hot, that's the top and bottom of it!

Pistol   Your expression is most apt. For rumness is here in plenty. Salvoes come and go. God's servants fall and die. [*Singing*]
And sword and shield
In bloody field
Will win immortal fame.

Boy   I wish I were in a tavern in London. I'd swap all my fame for a tankard of ale, and safety.

Pistol   I too! [*Singing*]
If wishes had their way with me
My purpose would not fail with me
It's there that I would go.

Boy   [*singing*] *As surely*
But not as purely
As a bird sings on a bough!

[**Captain Fluellen**, *a fiery Welshman, enters angrily*]

Fluellen   Up to the breach, you dogs! Get going, you turds!

[*He beats them energetically*]

Pistol   Be merciful, great warlord, to us mere mortals!
Subdue your rage, subdue your manly rage!
Subdue your rage, great warlord! Old chap, restrain yourself! Gently now, dear boy!

Nym   This is very rum! Your honour's in a right rummy mood.

[*They all go except the* **Boy**]

30 **Boy**   As young as I am, I have observed these three
swashers. I am boy to them all three, but all they three,
though they should serve me, could not be man to me,
for indeed three such antics do not amount to a man.
For Bardolph, he is white-livered and red-faced – by the
35 means whereof a faces it out, but fights not. For Pistol,
he hath a killing tongue and a quiet sword – by the
means whereof a breaks words, and keeps whole
weapons. For Nym, he hath heard that men of few
words are the best men, and therefore he scorns to say
40 his prayers, lest a should be thought a coward. But his
few bad words are matched with as few good deeds – for
a never broke any man's head but his own, and that
was against a post, when he was drunk. They will steal
anything, and call it purchase. Bardolph stole a lute
45 case, bore it twelve leagues, and sold it for three
halfpence. Nym and Bardolph are sworn brothers in
filching, and in Calais they stole a fire shovel. I knew by
that piece of service the men would carry coals. They
would have me as familiar with men's pockets as their
50 gloves or their handkerchiefs – which makes much
against my manhood, if I should take from another's
pocket to put into mine, for it is plain pocketing up of
wrongs. I must leave them, and seek some better service.
Their villainy goes against my weak stomach, and
55 therefore I must cast it up.

[*Exit*]

[*Enter* **Gower** *and* **Fluellen**, *meeting*]

Gower   Captain Fluellen, you must come presently to the
mines. The Duke of Gloucester would speak with you.

Boy   Young as I am, I've watched these three loudmouths. To all three I'm their servant; but all those three, even if they were my servants, they couldn't be my man-servants, 'cos three such clowns wouldn't make one real man. As for Bardolph, he's lily-livered and red-faced, so he can brazen things out but not fight. As for Pistol, he has a lethal tongue and an idle sword, so he fractures words and keeps his weapons in one piece. As for Nym, he has heard that men of few words are the toughest, so he scorns saying his prayers in case he's thought a coward. His few bad words are matched by as few good deeds. The only head he's ever broken is his own, and that was against a post when he was drunk. They'll steal anything and call it 'legit.' Bardolph stole a lute case, carried it twelve miles, and sold it for a few pence. Nym and Bardolph are sworn brothers – in pinching. In Calais they stole a fire shovel. I knew by that bit of military service they were men who'd do the dirty work! They'd have me in and out of pockets like men's gloves or their handkerchiefs. It goes against my masculinity, to be taking things from other men's pockets to put into mine: that's just like pocketing pride, which is unmanly. I must leave them and get a better job. Their villainy turns my stomach, so I must throw it all up.

[*He goes.* **Captain Gower**, *an English officer, enters, talking to* **Captain Fluellen**]

Gower   Captain Fluellen, you must come immediately to the tunnels. [*They were dug to place explosives under enemy walls, etc*] The Duke of Gloucester wishes to speak to you.

107

Fluellen   To the mines? Tell you the Duke it is not so goo
to come to the mines. For look you, the mines is not
60   according to the disciplines of the war. The concavities
of it is not sufficient. For look you, th'athversary, you
may discuss unto the Duke, look you, is digt himself four
yard under the countermines. By Cheshu, I think a will
blow up all, if there is not better directions.

65   **Gower**   The Duke of Gloucester, to whom the order of the
siege is given, is altogether directed by an Irishman, a
very valiant gentleman, i'faith.

Fluellen   It is Captain MacMorris, is it not?

Gower   I think it be.

70   **Fluellen**   By Cheshu, he is an ass, as in the world. I will
verify as much in his beard. He has no more directions
in the true disciplines of the wars, look you – of the
Roman disciplines – than is a puppy dog.

[*Enter* **Captain MacMorris** *and* **Captain Jamy**]

Gower   Here a comes, and the Scots captain, Captain
75   Jamy, with him.

Fluellen   Captain Jamy is a marvellous falorous
gentleman, that is certain, and of great expedition and
knowledge in th'ancient wars, upon my particular
knowledge of his directions. By Cheshu, he will maintain
80   his argument as well as any military man in the world,
in the disciplines of the pristine wars of the Romans.

Jamy   I say gud day, Captain Fluellen.

Fluellen   God-den to your worship, good Captain James.

Fluellen   To the tunnels? You can tell the Duke it's not pleasing for me to come to the tunnels. For, look you, the tunnels are not according to the correct tactics of warfare. The depth is insufficient. For look you: you can tell the Duke, look you, that the enemy has dug his countermines four yards under. By Jesu, I think I will blow them all up if there's no better planning.

Gower   The Duke of Gloucester, who is in charge of the siege, is advised by an Irishman; a very courageous gentleman, indeed.

Fluellen   That's Captain MacMorris, is it not?

Gower   I think it is.

Fluellen   By Jesu, he is an ass, if ever there was one. I will say so to his face. He has no more advice to give in the proper tactics of war, look you — of the Roman tactics — than has a puppy dog!

[**Captain MacMorris** *and* **Captain Jamy** *enter*]

Gower   Here he comes, and the Scots captain, Captain Jamy, with him.

Fluellen   Captain Jamy is an extremely valorous gentleman, that is certain, and of great expertise and knowledge about the classical wars which I know from his tactics. By Jesu, he'll defend his point of view concerning the ancient wars of the Romans as well as any military man in the world.

Jamy   Good day, Captain Fluellen!

Fluellen   Good evening to your worship, good Captain James!

Gower   How now, Captain MacMorris, have you quit the
85   mines? Have the pioneers given o'er?

MacMorris   By Chrish law, 'tish ill done. The work ish
give over, the trompet sound the retreat. By my hand I
swear, and my father's soul, the work ish ill done, it ish
give over. I would have blowed up the town, so Chrish
90   save me law, in an hour. Oh 'tish ill done, 'tish ill done,
by my hand 'tish ill done!

Fluellen   Captain MacMorris, I beseech you now, will you
voutsafe me, look you, a few disputations with you, as
partly touching or concerning the disciplines of the war,
95   the Roman wars, in the way of argument, look you, and
friendly communication? Partly to satisfy my opinion
and partly for the satisfaction, look you, of my mind. As
touching the direction of the military discipline, that is
the point.

100 **Jamy**   It sall be vary gud, gud feith, gud captains bath,
and I sall quite you with gud leve, as I may pick
occasion. That sall I, marry.

MacMorris   It is no time to discourse, so Chrish save me.
The day is hot, and the weather and the wars and the
105   King and the dukes. It is no time to discourse. The town
is besieched. An the trumpet call us to the breach, and
we talk and, be Chrish, do nothing, 'tis shame for us all.
So God sa' me, 'tis shame to stand still, it is shame by
my hand. And there is throats to be cut, and works to be
110   done, and there ish nothing done, so Chrish sa' me law!

Gower   Well now, Captain MacMorris: have you given up the tunnels? Have the pioneers stopped digging?

MacMorris   Be Jaisus, now – it's a bad business. The job's stopped and the trumpets have sounded retreat. I swear by my hand and on my father's soul, the job's ruined; it's stopped. I would have blowed up the town, so Christ save me now, in an hour! Oh, 'tis ruined, 'tis ruined!

Fluellen   Captain MacMorris, I beg you now. Will you grant me, look you, a few debating points with you, as partly with reference to, or concerning, the tactics of war – the Roman wars: by way of argument, look you, and friendly discussion? Partly to confirm my opinion, and partly for the satisfaction, look you, of my mind? With reference to the tactics of military discipline – that's my point.

Jamy   That would be very good; good indeed; good, captains both. And I'll give you a lively time given the chance. That I will, by the mother of God!

MacMorris   This is no time to be debating, Christ save me! It's a hectic day . . . what with the weather . . . and the war . . . and the King and the commanders . . . It's no time to be debating! The town is besieged . . . and the trumpets are calling us to the breach . . . while we talk, and by Christ, do nothing! It's a shame on us all! God save me, it's a shame to be standing still; it's a shame, by this hand! And there's throats to be cut, and work to be done – and there's nothing being done, so Christ save me now!

Jamy   By the mess, ere these eyes of mine take themselves
to slumber, ay'll de gud service, or I'll lie i'th
ground for it. I owe God a death, and I'll pay't as
valorously as I may, that sall I suirely do, that is the
115   brief and the long. Marry, I wad full fain heard some
question 'tween you twae.

Fluellen   Captain MacMorris, I think, look you, under
your correction, there is not many of your nation –

MacMorris   Of my nation? What ish my nation? Ish a
120   villain and a bastard and a knave and a rascal? What
ish my nation? Who talks of my nation?

Fluellen   Look you, if you take the matter otherwise than
is meant, Captain MacMorris, peradventure I shall think
you do not use me with that affability as in discretion
125   you ought to use me, look you, being as good a man as
yourself, both in the disciplines of war and in the
derivation of my birth, and in other particularities.

MacMorris   I do not know you so good a man as myself.
So Chrish save me, I will cut off your head.

130 **Gower**   Gentlemen both, you will mistake each other.

Jamy   Ah, that's a foul fault.

[*A parley is sounded*]

Gower   The town sounds a parley.

Fluellen   Captain MacMorris, when there is more better
opportunity to be required, look you, I will be so bold as
135   to tell you I know the disciplines of war. And there is an
end.

[*Exeunt*]

Jamy   By the holy mass, before I go to sleep tonight
   I'll do my share of fighting, or die in the attempt. I
   owe God a death, so I'll pay up as bravely as I can.
   That'll surely do. That's the long and short of it.
   God, I'd like to have heard you two argue it out.

Fluellen   Captain MacMorris: I think, look you —
   subject to your correction — that there are not many
   of your nation —

MacMorris   [*angry at being talked down to*] 'Of my
   nation'! What's 'my nation'? A villain and a bastard
   and a knave and a rascal? What's 'my nation'?
   Who's saying anything about my nation?

Fluellen   Look you, if you take the matter otherwise
   than was meant, Captain MacMorris, perhaps I shall
   think you are not treating me as courteously as you
   would be wise to treat me, look you, I being as
   good a man as yourself, both in war strategy and
   my country of birth, and in other respects.

MacMorris   I don't know that you are as good a man
   as myself. So, Christ save me, I'll cut your head off!

Gower   Gentlemen both, you will insist on
   misunderstanding each other!

Jamy   Och, that's a terrible fault.

   [*A trumpet is heard sounding a parley: an
   opportunity for the two sides to negotiate*]

Gower   The town is sounding a parley.

Fluellen   Captain MacMorris: at a more favourable
   opportunity, look you, I will be so bold as to tell you
   I know the strategies of war! I'll say no more.

   [*He goes*]

Scene 3

Before the gates of Harfleur. Enter **King Henry** *and all his train before the gates, the* **Governor** *and some citizens on the walls.*

King Henry   How yet resolves the Governor of the town?
This is the latest parle we will admit.
Therefore to our best mercy give yourselves,
Or like to men proud of destruction
5   Defy us to our worst. For as I am a soldier,
A name that in my thoughts becomes me best,
If I begin the batt'ry once again
I will not leave the half-achieved Harfleur
Till in her ashes she lie buried.
10   The gates of mercy shall be all shut up,
And the fleshed soldier, rough and hard of heart,
In liberty of bloody hand shall range
With conscience wide as hell, mowing like grass
Your fresh fair virgins and your flow'ring infants.
15   What is it then to me if impious war
Arrayed in flames like to the prince of fiends
Do with his smirched complexion all fell feats
Enlinked to waste and desolation?
What is't to me, when you yourselves are cause,
20   If your pure maidens fall into the hand
Of hot and forcing violation?
What rein can hold licentious wickedness
When down the hill he holds his fierce career?
We may as bootless spend our vain command
25   Upon th' enraged soldiers in their spoil
As send precepts to the leviathan
To come ashore. Therefore, you men of Harfleur,
Take pity of your town and of your people
Whiles yet my soldiers are in my command,
30   Whiles yet the cool and temperate wind of grace

Scene 3

Before the gates of Harfleur. A flourish of trumpets
heralds the arrival of **King Henry** *and his army*

King Henry   What has the Governor of the town
decided? This is the last ceasefire we will permit.
Therefore, surrender yourselves to our best mercy,
or like men who glory in destruction, defy us to do
our worst. For as I am a soldier – a name which I
think fits me best – if I begin the bombardment
once again, I will not leave the half-won Harfleur till
she lies buried in her ashes. The gates of mercy will
be slammed shut. The soldiers, hardened to killing,
rough and pitiless, will roam around with licence to
kill, unrestrained and conscienceless, mowing down
your lovely virgins and your growing infants. What
is it then to me if unholy war, dressed in flames like
Satan himself, with blackened features does every
cruel deed associated with devastation and
destruction? What is it to me, when you yourselves
are responsible, if your pure maidens fall into the
hands of vicious rapists? How can unbridled
wickedness be stopped once it has gathered
momentum? It would be as pointless to waste futile
commands on rampaging soldiers in the act of
pillage, as it would be to preach to the whale about
coming ashore. Therefore, you men of Harfleur, take
pity on your town and on your people, while I can
still control my soldiers, while calm and disciplined

O'erblows the filthy and contagious clouds
Of heady murder, spoil, and villainy.
If not – why, in a moment look to see
The blind and bloody soldier with foul hand
35 Defile the locks of your shrill-shrieking daughters;
Your fathers taken by the silver beards,
And their most reverend heads dashed to the walls;
Your naked infants spitted upon pikes,
Whiles the mad mothers with their howls confused
40 Do break the clouds, as did the wives of Jewry
At Herod's bloody-hunting slaughtermen.
What say you? Will you yield, and this avoid?
Or, guilty in defence, be thus destroyed?

Governor   Our expectation hath this day an end.
45 The Dauphin, whom of succours we entreated,
Returns us that his powers are not yet ready
To raise so great a siege. Therefore, great King,
We yield our town and lives to thy soft mercy.
Enter our gates, dispose of us and ours,
50 For we no longer are defensible.

King Henry   Open your gates.

[*Exit* **Governor**

Come, Uncle Exeter.
Go you and enter Harfleur. There remain,
And fortify it strongly 'gainst the French.
55 Use mercy to them all. For us, dear uncle,
The winter coming on, and sickness growing
Upon our soldiers, we will retire to Calais.
Tonight in Harfleur will we be your guest;
Tomorrow for the march are we addressed.

[*Flourish, and they enter the town*]

mercy transcends the viciousness of fanatical
murder, plunder and depravity! If not, why any
moment now expect to see the callous and
bloodstained soldier foully rape your shrill-shrieking
virgins; your fathers seized by their snow-white
beards and their most respected heads dashed
against the walls; your naked infants spitted upon
pikes, while their distraught mothers rend the
clouds with frenzied howls – as the Jewish women
did at Herod's bloodthirsty butchers. What do you
say? Will you surrender, and avoid all this? Or –
guilty in that you persist in your defence – will you
be destroyed as I've described?

[*The* **Governor of Harfleur** *appears on the town
walls*]

Governor   Today our hopes are ended. The Dauphin,
to whom we appealed for help, tells us that his
army is not yet ready to raise so great a siege.
Therefore, dread King, we surrender our town and
our lives to your tender mercy. Enter our gates;
dispose of us and ours; we can defend ourselves no
longer.

King Henry   Open your gates!

[*The* **Governor** *leaves to do so*]

Come, Uncle Exeter: go and enter Harfleur. Stay
there, and fortify it strongly against the French. Be
merciful to them all. As for us, dear uncle, with the
winter coming on and sickness spreading amongst
our troops, we will retire to Calais. Tonight, in
Harfleur, we will be your guest. Tomorrow we'll
march off.

[*The gates of Harfleur open. Trumpets sound as
they enter the town*]

117

Scene 4

Rouen. The French King's palace. Enter **Princess Katherine** *and* **Alice**.

Katherine   *Alice, tu as été en Angleterre, et tu bien parles le langage.*

Alice   *Un peu, madame.*

Katherine   *Je te prie, m'enseignez. Il faut que j'apprenne à*
5   *parler. Comment appelez-vous la main en Anglais?*

Alice   *La main? Elle est appelée* de hand.

Katherine   De hand. *Et les doigts?*

Alice   *Les doigts? Ma foi, j'oublie les doigts, mais je me souviendrai. Les doigts – je pense qu'ils sont appelés* de
10   fingres. *Oui,* de fingres.

Katherine   *La main,* de hand; *les doigts,* de fingres. *Je pense que je suis le bon écolier; j'ai gagné deux mots d'Anglais vîtement. Comment appelez-vous les ongles?*

Alice   *Les ongles? Nous les appelons* de nails.

15 **Katherine**   De nails. *Ecoutez – dites-moi si je parle bien*: de hand, de fingres, *et* de nails.

Alice   *C'est bien dit, madame. Il est fort bon Anglais.*

Katherine   *Dites-moi l'Anglais pour le bras.*

Alice   De arm, *madame.*

20 **Katherine**   *Et le coude?*

Alice   D'elbow.

Scene 4

The French Palace at Rouen. **Princess Katherine**
(daughter of **Charles***) is talking to* **Alice,** *her lady-in-waiting. French is, of course, the language she would naturally speak.*

Katherine   Alice, you've been to England, and you speak the language well.

Alice   A little, madam.

Katherine   Teach me, will you? I must learn to speak it. What do you call '*la main*' in English?

Alice   '*La main*'? It's called de hand.

Katherine   De hand. And '*les doigts*'?

Alice   '*Les doigts*'? Drat, I've forgotten '*les doigts*'! Oh, now I remember! '*Les doigts*' – I think they are called de fingers. Yes – de fingers.

Katherine   '*La main*' – de hand. '*Les doigts*' – de fingers. I think I'm a good scholar: I've learned two words of English very quickly. What do you call '*les ongles*'?

Alice   '*Les ongles*'? We call them de nails.

Katherine   De nails. Listen, tell me if I'm saying it right: de hand, de fingers, and de nails.

Alice   Very good, madam. That's really good English.

Katherine   Tell me the English for '*le bras*'.

Alice   De arma, madam.

Katherine   And '*le coude*'?

Alice   D'elbow.

Katherine   D'elbow. *Je m'en fais la répétition de tous les mots que vous m'avez appris dès à présent.*

Alice   *Il est trop difficile, madame, comme je pense.*

25 **Katherine**   *Excusez-moi, Alice, Ecoutez*: d'hand, de fingre, de nails, d'arma, de bilbow.

Alice   D'elbow, *madame.*

Katherine   *Oh Seigneur Dieu, je m'en oublie!* D'elbow. *Comment appelez-vous le col?*

30 **Alice**   De nick, *madame.*

Katherine   De nick. *Et le menton?*

Alice   De chin.

Katherine   De sin. *Le col*, de nick; *le menton*, de sin.

Alice   *Oui. Sauf votre honneur, en vérité vous prononcez les*
35   *mots aussi droit que les natifs d'Angleterre.*

Katherine   *Je ne doute point d'apprendre, par la grâce de Dieu, et en peu de temps.*

Alice   *N'avez-vous y déjà oublié ce que je vous ai enseigné?*

Katherine   *Non, et je reciterai à vous promptement*: d'hand,
40   de fingre, de mailes –

Alice   De nails, *madame.*

Katherine   De nails, de arm, de ilbow –

Alice   *Sauf votre honneur*, d'elbow.

Katherine   *Ainsi dis-je.* D'elbow, de nick, et de sin.
45   *Comment appelez-vous les pieds et la robe?*

Alice   De foot, *madame*, et de count.

Katherine   D'elbow. I'll repeat all the words you've taught me so far.

Alice   That's too hard, madam, I think.

Katherine   Excuse me, Alice. Listen: de hand; de finger; de nails; d'arma; de bilbow.

Alice   D'elbow, madam.

Katherine   Oh, dear God, I forgot! D'elbow. What do you call '*le col*'?

Alice   De nick, madam.

Katherine   And '*le menton*'?

Alice   De chin.

Katherine   De sin. '*Le col*' – de nick. '*Le menton*' – de sin.

Alice   Yes. With respect, you really do speak the words just like the natives of England.

Katherine   I'm sure I'll learn it, God willing, very quickly.

Alice   Haven't you already forgotten what I've taught you?

Katherine   No, and I'll recite them to you promptly: de hand, de finger, de mails –

Alice   De nails, madam.

Katherine   De nails, de arma, de ilbow –

Alice   With respect, d'elbow.

Katherine   That's what I said. D'elbow, de nick, and de sin. What do you call '*les pieds*' and '*la robe*'?

Alice   De foot, madam, and de cown.

121

Katherine   De foot *et* de count? *Oh Seigneur Dieu! Ils sont*
les mots de son mauvais, corruptible, gros, et impudique, et
non pour les dames d'honneur d'user: Je ne voudrais
50   *prononcer ces mots devant les seigneurs de France pour tout l*
monde. Foh! De foot *et* de count! *Néanmoins, je reciterai*
une autre fois ma leçon ensemble. D'hand, de fingre, de
nails, d'arm, d'elbow, de nick, de sin, de foot, de count.

Alice   *Excellent, madame!*

55 **Katherine**   *C'est assez pour une fois. Allons-nous à dîner.*

[*Exeun*

Scene 5

Enter the **King of France,** *the* **Dauphin,** *the* **Constable,** *the*
Duke of Britaine *and others.*

French King   'Tis certain he hath passed the River
Somme.

Constable   And if he be not fought withal, my lord,
Let us not live in France; let us quit all
5   And give our vineyards to a barbarous people.

Dauphin   *Oh Dieu vivant!* Shall a few sprays of us,
The emptying of our fathers' luxury,
Our scions, put in wild and savage stock,
Spirt up so suddenly into the clouds
10   And over-look their grafters?

Katherine   [*outraged; the two words are similar in sound to French swear-words*] De foot and de cown? Oh, dear God! They are naughty, indecent, gross and improper words and not for respectable girls to use. I wouldn't say those words in front of French gentlemen for all the world! Really! De foot and de cown! Nevertheless, I'll say my lesson one more time, all together: de hand, de finger, de nails, d'arma, d'elbow, de nick, de sin, de foot, de cown.

Alice   Excellent, madam!

Katherine   That's enough for one lesson. Let's go to dinner.

[*They go*]

Scene 5

The French palace at Rouen. **King Charles, The Dauphin, The Constable of France, The Duke of Britaine,** *and members of the court.*

King Charles   He's definitely crossed the River Somme.

Constable   If we don't fight him, my lord, let us not live in France. Let us quit everything and give our vineyards to barbarians!

Dauphin   Heavens alive! Shall a few offshoots of the French nation — the by-products of our forefathers' lust — our good buds grafted to the wild and savage Anglo-Saxons — sprout up so suddenly and loftily that they look down upon those who begot them?

Britaine   Normans, but bastard Normans, Norman
       bastards!
       Mort de ma vie, if they march along
       Unfought withal, but I will sell my dukedom
15   To buy a slobb'ry and a dirty farm
       In that nook-shotten isle of Albion.

Constable   *Dieu de batailles*! Where have they this mettle?
       Is not their climate foggy, raw, and dull,
       On whom as in despite the sun looks pale,
20   Killing their fruit with frowns? Can sodden water,
       A drench for sur-reined jades – their barley-broth –
       Decoct their cold blood to such valiant heat?
       And shall our quick blood, spirited with wine,
       Seem frosty? Oh for honour of our land
25   Let us not hang like roping icicles
       Upon our houses' thatch, whiles a more frosty people
       Sweat drops of gallant youth in our rich fields –
       Poor we may call them, in their native lords.

Dauphin   By faith and honour,
30   Our madams mock at us and plainly say
       Our mettle is bred out, and they will give
       Their bodies to the lust of English youth,
       To new-store France with bastard warriors.

Britaine   They bid us to the English dancing schools,
35   And teach lavoltas high and swift corantos,
       Saying our grace is only in our heels,
       And that we are most lofty runaways.

French King   Where is Montjoy the herald? Speed him
        hence.
40   Let him greet England with our sharp defiance.
       Up, princes, and with spirit of honour edged
       More sharper than your swords, hie to the field.

Britaine   They're Normans, but bastard Normans!
Norman bastards! Strike me dead – if they march
along unchallenged, then I'll sell my dukedom to
buy a dirty, mucky farm in that god-forsaken island
of Britain.

Constable   God of battles! Where do they get this
spirit from? Isn't their climate foggy, raw and dull?
The sun shines on them feebly, as if in contempt,
killing their fruit with frosts. Can stewed water, a
drink for clapped-out nags – their ale! – heat their
cold blood to such a courageous temperature? And
shall our lively blood, invigorated by wine, seem
cold? Oh, for the honour of our country: don't let's
hang like dripping icicles from roofs, while a colder-
blooded nation sweats gallant, youthful blood on
our rich fields which seem to deserve better owners
than our so-called nobles!

Dauphin   By my faith and honour, our lady-wives all
mock us, and bluntly say we're past it; and that
they'll mate with lusty English youths to re-stock
France with bastard soldiers.

Britaine   They tell us 'Go to English dancing-schools,
and teach them all the latest steps', saying our only
talents are in our feet, and we're just noble run-
aways.

King Charles   Where is Montjoy the herald? Send him
immediately. Let him tell England of our resolute
defiance. Up, princes, and with your Honour even
keener than your swords, make for the battlefield!

Charles Delabret, High Constable of France,
You Dukes of Orleans, Bourbon, and of Berri,
45 Alençon, Brabant, Bar, and Burgundy,
Jacques Chatillon, Rambures, Vaudemont,
Beaumont, Grandpré, Roussi, and Fauconbridge,
Foix, Lestrelles, Boucicault, and Charolois,
High dukes, great princes, barons, lords, and knights,
50 For your great seats now quit you of great shames.
Bar Harry England, that sweeps through our land
With pennons painted in the blood of Harfleur.
Rush on his host, as doth the melted snow
Upon the valleys, whose low vassal seat
55 The Alps doth spit and void his rheum upon.
Go down upon him, you have power enough,
And in a captive chariot into Rouen
Bring him our prisoner.

Constable   This becomes the great
60 Sorry am I his numbers are so few,
His soldiers sick and famished in their march,
For I am sure when he shall see our army
He'll drop his heart into the sink of fear
And for achievement, offer us his ransom.

65 **French King**   Therefore, Lord Constable, haste on
        Montjoy,
And let him say to England that we send
To know what willing ransom he will give.
Prince Dauphin, you shall stay with us in Rouen.

70 **Dauphin**   Not so, I do beseech your majesty.

French King   Be patient, for you shall remain with us.
Now forth, Lord Constable, and princes all,
And quickly bring us word of England's fall.

[Exeunt]

Charles Delabret, High Constable of France; you
Dukes of Orleans, Bourbon, Berri, Alençon, Brabant,
Bar, Burgundy; Jacques Chatillon, Rambures,
Vaudemont, Beaumont, Grandpré, Roussi,
Fauconbridge, Foix, Lestrelles, Boucicault,
Charolois; high dukes, great princes, barons, lords,
and knights, with your great ranks, now eliminate
great shame. Stop Harry England, who is sweeping
through our land with pennants stained with the
blood of Harfleur. Sweep down upon his army like
avalanches into valleys, used by the Alps as her
spittoons. Descend upon him – you have sufficient
forces – and bring him into Rouen as our prisoner,
captive in a chariot.

Constable   Words worthy of a great king! I'm only
sorry his forces are so small, with his soldiers sick
and hungry as they march. I'm certain that when he
sees our army, his heart will sink with fear, and he'll
offer us a ransom rather than a fight.

King Charles   Therefore, Lord Constable, hurry
Montjoy and let him tell England that we want to
know what ransom he will give. Prince Dauphin,
you will stay with us in Rouen.

Dauphin   Please, no – I beg Your Majesty!

King Charles   Patience, now, you shall remain with
us. Go now, Lord Constable and assembled princes,
and quickly bring us news of England's defeat.

   [*They all leave*]

Scene 6

The English camp at Picardy. Enter **Gower** *and* **Fluellen,** *meeting.*

Gower   How now, Captain Fluellen, come you from the bridge?

Fluellen   I assure you there is very excellent services committed at the bridge.

5 **Gower**   Is the Duke of Exeter safe?

Fluellen   The Duke of Exeter is as magnanimous as Agamemnon, and a man that I love and honour with my soul and my heart and my duty and my life and my living and my uttermost power. He is not, God be
10 praised and blessed, any hurt in the world, but keeps the bridge most valiantly, with excellent discipline. There is an ancient-lieutenant there at the pridge; I think in my very conscience he is as valiant a man as Mark Antony, and he is a man of no estimation in the world, but I did
15 see him do as gallant service.

Gower   What do you call him?

Fluellen   He is called Ancient Pistol.

Gower   I know him not.

[*Enter* **Pistol**]

Fluellen   Here is the man.

20 **Pistol**   Captain, I thee beseech to do me favours. The Duke of Exeter doth love thee well.

Fluellen   Ay, I praise God, and I have merited some love at his hands.

Scene 6

Near the bridge over the river Ternoise. **Captain Gower** *meets* **Captain Fluellen.**

Gower   Greetings, Captain Fluellen! Have you come from the bridge?

Fluellen   I assure you: there's been excellent work done at the bridge.

Gower   Is the Duke of Exeter safe?

Fluellen   The Duke of Exeter is as courageous as Agamemnon, and a man whom I love and honour with my heart and my soul and my duty and my life and my living and my utmost strength. He is not, God be praised and blessed, in any way injured. He holds the bridge most valiantly, with excellent discipline. There is an Ensign Lieutenant there at the bridge: I really believe him to be as valiant a man as Mark Antony, yet he is a man of no public renown. But I saw him do equally gallant service.

Gower   What's his name?

Fluellen   He's called Ensign Pistol.

Gower   I don't know him.

   [**Pistol** *enters*]

Fluellen   Here's the man!

Pistol   [*to* **Fluellen**] Captain, I do beseech you, a favour if you will. The Duke of Exeter is very fond of you —

Fluellen   Yes, praise God, and I've earned some affection from him!

25 **Pistol** Bardolph, a soldier firm and sound of heart,
        Of buxom valour, hath by cruel fate
        And giddy Fortune's furious fickle wheel,
        That goddess blind
        That stands upon the rolling restless stone –

30 **Fluellen** By your patience, Ancient Pistol: Fortune is
        painted blind, with a muffler afore her eyes, to signify to
        you that Fortune is blind. And she is painted also with a
        wheel, to signify to you – which is the moral of it – that
        she is turning and inconstant and mutability and
35   variation. And her foot, look you, is fixed upon a
        spherical stone, which rolls and rolls and rolls. In good
        truth, the poet makes a most excellent description of it:
        Fortune is an excellent moral.

    Pistol Fortune is Bardolph's foe and frowns on him.
40   For he hath stolen a pax,
        And hanged must a be. A damned death –
        Let gallows gape for dog, let man go free,
        And let not hemp his windpipe suffocate.
        But Exeter hath given the doom of death
45   For pax of little price.
        Therefore go speak, the Duke will hear thy voice,
        And let not Bardolph's vital thread be cut
        With edge of penny cord and vile reproach.
        Speak, captain, for his life, and I will thee requite.

50 **Fluellen** Ancient Pistol, I do partly understand your
        meaning.

    Pistol Why then rejoice therefore.

    Fluellen Certainly, Ancient, it is not a thing to rejoice at.
        For if, look you, he were my own brother, I would desire
55   the Duke to use his good pleasure, and put him to
        execution. For discipline ought to be used.

Pistol   Bardolph – a soldier firm and stout of heart, and of outstanding valour – has, by cruel fate and the foolish fickle wheel of flighty fortune – that blind goddess who stands upon a rolling, ever-turning stone –

Fluellen   With respect, Ensign Pistol. Fortune is depicted as blind by her wearing a blindfold – to signify to you that she is blind. And she is also painted with a wheel, to signify to you – which is the moral of it – that she turns, and is inconstant; change and variation. And her foot, look you, stands upon a spherical stone, which rolls and rolls and rolls. Really, poets make good use of it: Fortune is an excellent symbolic figure.

Pistol   Fortune is Bardolph's foe, and frowns upon him. He has stolen a holy tablet from a church, and he must hang. A ghastly death! Let gallows hang a dog; let man go free – and let no cord his windpipe suffocate. Exeter has sentenced him to death, for theft of tablet with a value small. Therefore, speak up on his behalf; the Duke will hear your plea. Let not Bardolph's life conclude by means of low-priced rope, and odious slur. Speak, captain, for his life! I will you repay!

Fluellen   Ensign Pistol: I understood part of what you said –

Pistol   Why, then, rejoice!

Fluellen   Actually, Ensign, it's not something to rejoice at. Because look you, if he were my own brother, I would want the Duke to carry out his intentions and execute him. We've got to have discipline!

Pistol   Die and be damned! and figo for thy friendship.

Fluellen   It is well.

Pistol   The fig of Spain.

60 **Fluellen**   Very good.   [*Exit*

Gower   Why, this is an arrant counterfeit rascal: I
remember him now. A bawd, a cutpurse.

Fluellen   I'll assure you, a uttered as prave words at the
pridge as you shall see in a summer's day. But it is very
65   well. What he has spoke to me, that is well, I warrant
you, when time is serve.

Gower   Why 'tis a gull, a fool, a rogue, that now and then
goes to the wars, to grace himself at his return into
London under the form of a soldier. And such fellows
70   are perfect in the great commanders' names, and they
will learn you by rote where services were done – at such
and such a sconce, at such a breach, at such a convoy,
who came off bravely, who was shot, who disgraced,
what terms the enemy stood on – and this they con
75   perfectly in the phrase of war, which they trick up with
new-tuned oaths. And what a beard of the General's cut
and a horrid suit of the camp will do among foaming
bottles and ale-washed wits is wonderful to be thought
on. But you must learn to know such slanders of this
80   age, or else you may be marvellously mistook.

Pistol   Die and be damned to you! A fig for your friendship!

[*Combined with a rude sign, 'fig' was insulting*]

Fluellen   [*refusing to be provoked*] That's all right.

Pistol   A Spanish fig! [*These were usually poisoned*]

Fluellen   Very good.

[**Fluellen** *refuses to react.* **Pistol** *leaves, defeated*]

Gower   Why, is this the Ensign you told me about? I remember him now. He's a pimp and a pickpocket.

Fluellen   Believe me, he spoke words at the bridge as brave as you have ever heard. But that's all right. What he said to me, that's all right, I assure you, till the right time comes . . .

Gower   Why, he's a simpleton, a fool, a rogue! He goes to the wars now and again so he can return to London and boast he has been a soldier. Such fellows know all the great commanders' names word-perfect. They can recite by heart where they were supposed to be in action – at such-and-such a fort, at such-and-such a breach, at such-and-such a march, who did brave work, who was shot, who disgraced, what terms the enemy laid down. All this they learn perfectly, using military language, which they make more convincing with the latest oaths. It's amazing what a beard styled like the General's, and an unkempt uniform, can do amongst flowing ale and drunken clots! But you must learn to recognise the riff-raff of our times or else you can be badly deceived.

Fluellen I tell you what, Captain Gower. I do perceive he is not the man that he would gladly make show to the world he is. If I find a hole in his coat, I will tell him my mind.

[*A drum is heard*]

85 Hark you, the King is coming, and I must speak with him from the pridge.

[*Enter* **King Henry** *and his poor soldiers, with drum and colours*]

God pless your majesty!

King Henry How now, Fluellen, came'st thou from the bridge?

90 **Fluellen** Ay, so please your majesty. The Duke of Exeter has very gallantly maintained the pridge. The French is gone off, look you, and there is gallant and most prave passages. Marry, th'athversary was have possession of the pridge, but he is enforced to retire, and the Duke of
95 Exeter is master of the pridge. I can tell your majesty, the Duke is a prave man.

King Henry What men have you lost, Fluellen?

Fluellen The perdition of th'athversary hath been very great, very reasonably great. Marry for my part I think
100 the Duke hath lost never a man, but one that is like to be executed for robbing a church, one Bardolph, if your majesty know the man. His face is all bubukles and whelks and knobs and flames o'fire, and his lips blows at his nose, and it is like a coal of fire, sometimes plue
105 and sometimes red. But his nose is executed, and his fire's out.

Fluellen I tell you what, Captain Gower: I see now he isn't the man he pretends to be. If I get a suitable opportunity, I will give him a piece of my mind.

[*A drum is heard*]

Listen – the King is coming. I must speak to him about the bridge.

[**King Henry** *and his bedraggled soldiers enter*]

God bless Your Majesty!

King Henry Greetings, Fluellen. Have you come from the bridge?

Fluellen Yes, so please Your Majesty. The Duke of Exeter has very gallantly held the bridge. The French have gone, look you, and there has been gallant and brave fighting. Indeed, the enemy had possession of the bridge, but he's been forced to retreat and the Duke of Exeter has taken it over. I can tell your majesty: the Duke is a brave man.

King Henry How many men have you lost, Fluellen?

Fluellen The enemy losses have been very great, quite considerable . . . Indeed, as far as I know the Duke hasn't lost a single man, except one who is going to be executed for robbing a church: one Bardolph, if your majesty knows the man. [*He does: in former days they drank and got up to mischief together*] His face is all boils and pimples and lumps and red patches, and his lips blow his breath towards his nose: it's like a coal fire, sometimes blue and sometimes red. But they've slit his nose, and his fire is out.

King Henry   We would have all such offenders so cut off,
and we here give express charge that in our marches
through the country there be nothing compelled from the
110 villages, nothing taken but paid for, none of the French
upbraided or abused in disdainful language. For when
lenity and cruelty play for a kingdom, the gentler
gamester is the soonest winner.

[*Tucket. Enter* **Montjoy**]

Montjoy   You know me by my habit.

115 **King Henry**   Well then, I know thee. What shall I know of
thee?

Montjoy   My master's mind.

King Henry   Unfold it.

Montjoy   Thus says my King:
120 'Say thou to Harry of England, though we seemed dead
we did but sleep. Advantage is a better soldier than
rashness. Tell him, we could have rebuked him at
Harfleur, but that we thought not good to bruise an
injury till it were full ripe. Now we speak upon our cue,
125 and our voice is imperial. England shall repent his folly,
see his weakness, and admire our sufferance. Bid him
therefore consider of his ransom, which must proportion
the losses we have borne, the subjects we have lost, the
disgrace we have digested – which in weight to re-
130 answer, his pettiness would bow under. For our losses,
his exchequer is too poor; for th'effusion of our blood,
the muster of his kingdom too faint a number; and for

King Henry   We would have all such offenders
similarly despatched, and we here give specific
orders that in our marches through the country,
nothing shall be extorted from the villages; nothing
taken that isn't paid for; none of the French berated
or abused in disdainful language. When kindness
and cruelty compete for a kingdom, the gentler
player gets there first.

[*A fanfare.* **Montjoy** *the* **Herald** *enters*]

Montjoy   You know me by my uniform.

King Henry   Well then, I know you. What shall I know
from you?

Montjoy   My master's decision.

King Henry   Reveal it.

Montjoy   This is what my King says: [*he reads from a
scroll*]

'Tell Harry of England that though we seemed dead,
we were only sleeping. Discretion is a better soldier
than valour. Tell him we could have repulsed him at
Harfleur, but we thought it better not to squeeze the
boil till it had come to a head. Now we are ready to
speak, and our voice is that of authority. Harry of
England shall repent his folly, see his weakness,
and marvel at our patience. Instruct him therefore to
give thought to his ransom-money, which must
relate to the losses we have suffered, the subjects
we have lost, and the disgrace that we have
stomached – which to compensate in money terms
would be more than a man of his small substance
could repay. His exchequer is too poor to
recompense us for our losses; the population of his

137

our disgrace, his own person kneeling at our feet but a
weak and worthless satisfaction. To this add defiance,
135 and tell him for conclusion he hath betrayed his
followers, whose condemnation is pronounced.'
So far my King and master; so much my office.

King Henry   What is thy name? I know thy quality.

Montjoy   Montjoy.

140 **King Henry**   Thou dost thy office fairly. Turn thee back
And tell thy king I do not seek him now,
But could be willing to march on to Calais
Without impeachment, for to say the sooth –
Though 'tis no wisdom to confess so much
145 Unto an enemy of craft and vantage –
My people are with sickness much enfeebled,
My numbers lessened, and those few I have
Almost no better than so many French:
Who when they were in health I tell thee herald,
150 I thought upon one pair of English legs
Did march three Frenchmen. Yet forgive me, God,
That I do brag thus. This your air of France
Hath blown that vice in me. I must repent.
Go, therefore, tell thy master here I am;
155 My ransom is this frail and worthless trunk,
My army but a weak and sickly guard.
Yet, God before, tell him we will come on,
Though France himself and such another neighbour
Stand in our way. There's for thy labour, Montjoy.
160 Go bid thy master well advise himself.
If we may pass, we will; if we be hindered,

kingdom too insignificant to cover the spilling of
our blood; and as for our disgrace, it would be an
inadequate and worthless satisfaction to have his
own person kneeling at our feet. To this add
defiance: and tell him in conclusion that he has
betrayed his followers, whose fate is sealed.'

So says my King and master. [*He rolls up his scroll*]
So much is my duty.

King Henry   What is your name? I know your
occupation.

Montjoy   Montjoy.

King Henry   You do your job well. Go back and tell
your King I do not seek a confrontation with him
now, but would prefer to march on to Calais
unchallenged. Frankly – though it isn't wise to
confess so much to an enemy who's both cunning
and advantageously situated – my people are in
poor condition through sickness; my numbers are
depleted; and the few I have are hardly any better
than the same number of French. When they were
fit – believe me, herald – I thought one pair of
English legs carried the equivalent of three
Frenchmen. But forgive me, God, for boasting like
this. I have caught the habit from your French air. I
must repent. Go, therefore, and tell your master I
am here. My ransom is this frail and worthless
body; my army just a weak and sickly bodyguard.
Yet, God willing, tell him we'll press on even
though the French King himself and a neighbour
just as powerful should stand in our way. (*He hands*
Montjoy *a purse*] There's something for your
trouble, Montjoy. Go and tell your master to think
again. If we may continue, we will. If we are

We shall your tawny ground with your red blood
Discolour. And so, Montjoy, fare you well.
The sum of all our answer is but this:
165 We would not seek a battle as we are,
Nor as we are we say we will not shun it.
So tell your master.

Montjoy   I shall deliver so. Thanks to your highness.

[*Exit*

Gloucester   I hope they will not come upon us now.

170 **King Henry**   We are in God's hand, brother, not in theirs.
March to the bridge. It now draws toward night.
Beyond the river we'll encamp ourselves,
And on tomorrow bid them march away.

[*Exeunt*

Scene 7

The French camp near Agincourt. Enter the **Constable,**
Rambures, *the* **Dauphin,** *the* **Duke of Orleans** *and others.*

Constable   Tut! I have the best armour of the world.
Would it were day!

Orleans   You have an excellent armour. But let my horse
have his due.

5 **Constable**   It is the best horse of Europe.

Orleans   Will it never be morning?

hindered, we'll dye your tawny earth with your red blood. And so, Montjoy: fare you well. To sum up our answer: we would not seek a battle as we are, but being as we are, we would not shun one either. Tell your master that.

Montjoy   I'll do that. Thanks to Your Highness.

[*He goes*]

Gloucester   I hope they won't attack us now.

King Henry   We are in God's hand, brother, not in theirs. March to the bridge. Night approaches. We'll camp on the other side of the river, and give them marching orders tomorrow.

[*They go*]

Scene 7

The French camp at night. The nobles await the forthcoming battle near Agincourt. Amongst those present are the **Dauphin**, *the* **Constable of France**, *the* **Duke of Orleans**, *and* **Lord Rambures**. *They are killing time, watching for daylight.*

Constable   Tut, I have the best armour in the world! I wish it was day!

Orleans   You have excellent armour. But give my horse his due.

Constable   It's the best horse in Europe.

Orleans   Will it never be morning . . .?

Dauphin My lord of Orleans and my Lord High
Constable, you talk of horse and armour?

Orleans You are as well provided of both as any prince in
10 the world.

Dauphin What a long night is this! I will not change my
horse with any that treads but on four pasterns. *Ça, ha*!
He bounds from the earth as if his entrails were hares –
le cheval volant, the Pegasus, *qui a les narines de feu*!
15 When I bestride him, I soar, I am a hawk; he trots the
air, the earth sings when he touches it, the basest horn
of his hoof is more musical than the pipe of Hermes.

Orleans He's of the colour of the nutmeg.

Dauphin And of the heat of the ginger. It is a beast for
20 Perseus. He is pure air and fire, and the dull elements of
earth and water never appear in him, but only in patient
stillness while his rider mounts him. He is indeed a
horse, and all other jades you may call beasts.

Constable Indeed, my lord, it is a most absolute and
25 excellent horse.

Dauphin It is the prince of palfreys. His neigh is like the
bidding of a monarch, and his countenance enforces
homage.

Orleans No more, cousin.

30 **Dauphin** Nay, the man hath no wit, that cannot from the
rising of the lark to the lodging of the lamb vary
deserved praise on my palfrey. It is a theme as fluent as
the sea. Turn the sands into eloquent tongues, and my

Dauphin   My Lord of Orleans and my Lord High
   Constable: if it's horses and armour you are talking
   about –

Orleans   You are as well equipped as any prince in
   the world.

Dauphin   What a long night this is! I wouldn't change
   my horse for anything else on four legs. He bounds
   from the earth as if he had a stomachful of hares.
   The flying horse – Pegasus – with the fiery nostrils!
   When I sit astride him, I soar! I'm a hawk! He trots
   on air; the earth sings when he touches it. The
   sound of his hooves is more musical than the pipe
   of Hermes. [*It put Argus, who had a hundred eyes,
   to sleep*]

Orleans   He's nutmeg-coloured. [*Thought to be the
   sign of a placid horse*]

Dauphin   But with plenty of ginger! He's a beast fit
   for Perseus. [*He cut off Medusa's head: Pegasus
   sprang from her blood*] He's pure air and fire; the
   placid elements of earth and water are absent,
   except when his rider mounts him, then he's patient
   and still. He is indeed a horse. All other nags are
   just 'beasts'.

Constable   Indeed, my lord. It's an absolutely
   marvellous horse.

Dauphin   He is the prince of steeds. His neigh is regal,
   and his looks command respect.

Orleans   That'll do, cousin.

Dauphin   Really, the man who can't eulogise on my
   steed from larkrise till the lamb goes to bed has no
   brains. It's a theme as infinite as the vast sea; if the

143

horse is argument for them all. 'Tis a subject for a
35 sovereign to reason on, and for a sovereign's sovereign to
ride on, and for the world, familiar to us and unknown,
to lay apart their particular functions, and wonder at
him. I once writ a sonnet in his praise, and began thus:
'Wonder of nature! –'

40 **Orleans**   I have heard a sonnet begin so to one's mistress.

Dauphin   Then did they imitate that which I composed to
my courser, for my horse is my mistress.

Orleans   Your mistress bears well.

Dauphin   Me well, which is the prescribed praise and
45 perfection of a good and particular mistress.

Constable   Nay, for methought yesterday your mistress
shrewdly shook your back.

Dauphin   So perhaps did yours.

Constable   Mine was not bridled.

50 **Dauphin**   Oh then belike she was old and gentle, and you
rode like a kern of Ireland, your French hose off, and in
your strait strossers.

Constable   You have good judgement in horsemanship.

Dauphin   Be warned by me then: they that ride so, and
55 ride not warily, fall into foul bogs. I had rather have my
horse to my mistress.

shores could speak, my horse would be praised by every grain of sand. He's a subject for a sovereign to think about; for a sovereign's sovereign to ride upon; and for everyone – friends and strangers – to lay aside whatever they are doing to marvel at! I once wrote a sonnet in praise of him, which began like this: 'Wonder of nature –'

Orleans   I've heard a sonnet to one's mistress begin like that . . .

Dauphin   Then it was a copy of what I composed about my charger, because my horse is my mistress.

Orleans   Your mistress is a good mount . . .

Dauphin   For me personally – the highest recommendation is a good and exclusive mistress . . .

Constable   But I thought your mistress gave you a rough ride yesterday?

Dauphin   So did yours, I think.

Constable   Mine wasn't the bridled variety.

Dauphin   Then she was probably old and knackered, and you rode her like an Irish peasant: your trousers off, wearing just your underpants.

Constable   You're a good judge of horse. [*Perhaps he means 'whores'?*]

Dauphin   Take warning from me, then: those who ride like that, and don't ride carefully, end up clapped out. I prefer to have my horse as my mistress.

Constable   I had as lief have my mistress a jade.

Dauphin   I tell thee, Constable, my mistress wears his own hair.

60 **Constable**   I could make as true a boast as that, if I had a sow to my mistress.

Dauphin   '*Le chien est retourné à son propre vomissement, et la truie lavée au bourbier.*' Thou makest use of anything.

65 **Constable**   Yet do I not use my horse for my mistress, or any such proverb so little kin to the purpose.

Rambures   My Lord Constable, the armour that I saw in your tent tonight, are those stars or suns upon it?

Constable   Stars, my lord.

70 **Dauphin**   Some of them will fall tomorrow, I hope.

Constable   And yet my sky shall not want.

Dauphin   That may be, for you bear a many superfluously, and 'twere more honour some were away.

Constable   Even as your horse bears your praises, who
75   would trot as well were some of your brags dismounted.

Dauphin   Would I were able to load him with his desert! Will it never be day? I will trot tomorrow a mile, and my way shall be paved with English faces.

Constable   I will not say so, for fear I should be faced out
80   of my way. But I would it were morning, for I would fain be about the ears of the English.

Rambures   Who will go to hazard with me for twenty prisoners?

Constable   I'd just as soon have my mistress a nag.

Dauphin   I tell you what, Constable: my mistress does wear his own hair.

Constable   I could say the same if my mistress happened to be a sow.

Dauphin   'The dog returns to its vomit, and the clean sow to its muck.' You're not choosy.

Constable   Yet I don't substitute my horse for my mistress, or quote irrelevant proverbs.

Rambures   My Lord Constable. The armour I saw in your tent tonight: are those stars or suns on it?

Constable   Stars, my lord.

Dauphin   Some of them will have disappeared by tomorrow, I trust.

Constable   There'll be plenty left.

Dauphin   No doubt. You have far too many; fewer would be more discreet.

Constable   Like praises and your horse. It would trot just as well if some of your boasts dismounted.

Dauphin   Would that I could do his wit justice! Will it never be day? I'll trot a mile tomorrow, and my route will be paved with English faces.

Constable   I wouldn't say that, in case I had to detour, and lost face. But I wish it were morning: I want to start giving those English a good hiding.

Rambures   Who'll risk a bet? I say I'll take twenty prisoners!

Constable   You must first go yourself to hazard, ere you
85   have them.

Dauphin   'Tis midnight. I'll go arm myself.

[*Exit*]

Orleans   The Dauphin longs for morning.

Rambures   He longs to eat the English.

Constable   I think he will eat all he kills.

90 **Orleans**   By the white hand of my lady, he's a gallant
prince.

Constable   Swear by her foot, that she may tread out the
oath.

Orleans   He is simply the most active gentleman of
95   France.

Constable   Doing is activity, and he will still be doing.

Orleans   He never did harm that I heard of.

Constable   Nor will do none tomorrow. He will keep that
good name still.

100 **Orleans**   I know him to be valiant.

Constable   I was told that by one that knows him better
than you.

Orleans   What's he?

Constable   Marry, he told me so himself, and he said he
105   cared not who knew it.

Orleans   He needs not; it is no hidden virtue in him.

Constable   Before you capture them, you'll need to take some risks yourself.

Dauphin   It's midnight. I'll put my armour on.

[*He goes*]

Orleans   The Dauphin longs for morning.

Rambures   He longs to eat the English.

Constable   [*drily*] I think he'll eat all he kills . . .

Orleans   [*loyally*] By my lady's white hand, he's a gallant prince!

Constable   Why don't you swear by her foot? Then she could express her disagreement by stamping it.

Orleans   He is simply the most active gentleman in France.

Constable   Breeding is activity. He's forever at that.

Orleans   He has done nobody any harm that I know of.

Constable   Nor will he tomorrow. He'll be true to form.

Orleans   He's brave. I know that.

Constable   I was told the same by someone who knows him better than you do.

Orleans   Who's that?

Constable   Why, he told me so himself, and he said he didn't care who knew it.

Orleans   He doesn't need to. It's not a hidden virtue.

Constable   By my faith, sir, but it is. Never anybody saw
it but his lackey. 'Tis a hooded valour, and when it
appears it will bate.

110 **Orleans**   'Ill will never said well'.

Constable   I will cap that proverb with 'There is flattery
in friendship'.

Orleans   And I will take up that with 'Give the devil his
due'.

115 **Constable**   Well placed! There stands your friend for the
devil. Have at the very eye of that proverb with 'A pox
of the devil!'

Orleans   You are the better at proverbs by how much 'a
fool's bolt is soon shot'.

120 **Constable**   You have shot over.

Orleans   'Tis not the first time you were overshot.

[*Enter a* **Messenger**]

Messenger   My Lord High Constable, the English lie
within fifteen hundred paces of your tents.

Constable   Who hath measured the ground?

125 **Messenger** The Lord Grandpré.

Constable   A valiant and most expert gentleman.

[*Exit* **Messenger**]

Would it were day! Alas, poor Harry of England. He
longs not for the dawning as we do.

150

Constable   'Faith, sir, it is: apart from his valet, nobody has ever had experience of it in action. His valour is kept under cover; when the wraps are off, it won't look very impressive.

Orleans   'Ill will never spoke well'.

Constable   I'll cap that proverb with 'There's flattery in friendship'.

Orleans   And I'll take that up with 'Give the devil his due'.

Constable   Well said, your friend is the devil! A bull's eye with 'A pox on the Devil'.

Orleans   You are better than I am at proverbs by the extent to which 'A fool shoots before he takes his aim'.

Constable   I'm outgunned!

Orleans   It's not the first time you were wide of the mark.

[A **Messenger** *enters*]

Messenger   My Lord High Constable, the English are camped within fifteen hundred paces of your tents.

Constable   Who has measured the distance?

Messenger   The Lord Granpré.

Constable   A valiant and very expert gentleman . . .

[*The* **Messenger** *leaves*]

Would it were day! Alas, poor Harry of England. He doesn't long for dawn as we do.

Orleans   What a wretched and peevish fellow is this King
130   of England, to mope with his fat-brained followers so far
out of his knowledge.

Constable   If the English had any apprehension, they
would run away.

Orleans   That they lack; for if their heads had any
135   intellectual armour, they could never wear such heavy
head-pieces.

Rambures   That island of England breeds very valiant
creatures. Their mastiffs are of unmatchable courage.

Orleans   Foolish curs, that run winking into the mouth of
140   a Russian bear, and have their heads crushed like rotten
apples. You may as well say, 'That's a valiant flea that
dare eat his breakfast on the lip of a lion.'

Constable   Just, just. And the men do sympathize with the
mastiffs in robustious and rough coming on, leaving their
145   wits with their wives. And then, give them great meals of
beef, and iron and steel, they will eat like wolves and
fight like devils.

Orleans   Ay, but these English are shrewdly out of beef.

Constable   Then shall we find tomorrow they have only
150   stomachs to eat, and none to fight. Now is it time to
arm. Come, shall we about it?

Orleans   It is now two o'clock. But let me see – by ten
We shall have each a hundred Englishmen.

[*Exeunt*]

Orleans   What a wretched and idiotic fellow this King of England is, to be mooning around with his thick-headed followers so far from home.

Constable   If the English had any sense, they'd run away.

Orleans   They haven't got any. If they had brains, they couldn't bear to wear such heavy helmets.

Rambures   That island of England breeds very brave animals. Their mastiffs are unequalled for courage.

Orleans   Foolish dogs: they close their eyes and run straight into the mouths of Russian bears, and have their heads crushed like rotten apples. You might as well say 'It's a brave flea that dares to eat its breakfast on a lion's lip'.

Constable   A fair point. The men resemble the mastiffs in harebrained and reckless aggressiveness. They leave their brains behind with their wives. If you give them great meals of beef, and iron, and steel, they'll eat like wolves and fight like devils.

Orleans   Yes, but these English are grievously short of beef.

Constable   Then tomorrow we'll discover they have stomachs for food, but not fighting. Now it's time to put our armour on. Shall we?

Orleans   It's two o'clock. Let me see – by ten we'll each have taken a hundred Englishmen.

   [*They go*]

Act four

Enter **Chorus**

Chorus   Now entertain conjecture of a time
When creeping murmur and the poring dark
Fills the wide vessel of the universe.
From camp to camp through the foul womb of night
5   The hum of either army stilly sounds,
That the fixed sentinels almost receive
The secret whispers of each other's watch.
Fire answers fire, and through their paly flames
Each battle sees the other's umbered face.
10   Steed threatens steed, in high and boastful neighs
Piercing the night's dull ear, and from the tents
The armourers, accomplishing the knights,
With busy hammers closing rivets up,
Give dreadful note of preparation.
15   The country cocks do crow, the clocks do toll
And the third hour of drowsy morning name.
Proud of their numbers and secure in soul,
The confident and overlusty French
Do the low-rated English play at dice,
20   And chide the cripple tardy-gaited night,
Who like a foul and ugly witch doth limp
So tediously away. The poor condemned English,
Like sacrifices, by their watchful fires
Sit patiently and inly ruminate
25   The morning's danger; and their gesture sad,
Investing lank-lean cheeks and war-worn coats,
Presenteth them unto the gazing moon
So many horrid ghosts. Oh now, who will behold

Act four

*The **Announcer** returns to the stage.*

Announcer   Now imagine a time when hushed voices
fill the entire universe. From camp to camp, through
the black void, the hum of both the armies softly
sounds. The men on guard can almost hear each
other as they whisper secretly on watch. Fires burn
on both sides of the battle lines; and by their dim
flames each army sees the other's shadowy face.
Horse threatens horse with high-pitched, boastful
neighs that pierce the silence of the night; and from
the tents the armourers, fitting out the knights, give
fearful warnings of preparation, as they hammer
busily away, closing up rivets. The country cocks
crow. The clocks strike, and tell us it is three o'clock.
Proud of their superior numbers, and secure in
heart, the confident and overactive French play dice,
using the low-rated Englishmen as their stakes,
chiding the crippled, slow-paced night that like a
hideous and ugly witch limps away so tediously.
The poor, condemned English, like sacrifices, sit
patiently by their watchfires and brood about the
danger of the morning; and their drooping
postures, together with hollow cheeks and war-
worn coats, make them seem so many fearful
ghosts in the moonlight. Now, whoever sees the

155

The royal captain of this ruined band
30 Walking from watch to watch, from tent to tent,
Let him cry, 'Praise and glory on his head!
For forth he goes and visits all his host,
Bids them good-morrow with a modest smile
And calls them brothers, friends, and countrymen.
35 Upon his royal face there is no note
How dread an army hath enrounded him;
Nor doth he dedicate one jot of colour
Unto the weary and all-watched night,
But freshly looks and overbears attaint
40 With cheerful semblance and sweet majesty,
That every wretch, pining and pale before,
Beholding him, plucks comfort from his looks.
A largess universal, like the sun,
His liberal eye doth give to everyone,
45 Thawing cold fear, that mean and gentle all
Behold, as may unworthiness define,
A little touch of Harry in the night.
And so our scene must to the battle fly,
Where oh for pity! we shall much disgrace,
50 With four or five most vile and ragged foils,
Right ill-disposed in brawl ridiculous,
The name of Agincourt. Yet sit and see,
Minding true things by what their mock'ries be.

[*Exit*]

royal captain of this ruined band walking from
guard to guard, from tent to tent, let him cry 'Praise
and glory on his head!' Because out he goes and
visits all his army, bidding them 'Good morning'
with a modest smile, and calling them 'brothers',
'friends' and 'fellow-countrymen'. On his royal face
is no hint of the formidable army that has encircled
him. Nor does he concede one jot of colour to the
weary and suspenseful night. Instead, he looks fresh
and conceals his exhaustion beneath cheerful looks
and graciousness, so that every wretched man who
sees him, though low-spirited and pale before, takes
comfort from his looks. Acknowledging everyone,
he spreads a universal warmth, like the sun,
thawing cold fear; and men of all ranks behold – if I
may put it this way – a fleeting glimpse of Harry in
the night.

And so our scene must change now to the battle,
where – oh dear! – we'll much disgrace the name of
Agincourt with four or five bedraggled swords
ineptly crossed in mock battle . . . Keep your seats
and watch: imagining the real with the help of
shabby imitations!

[*He goes*]

Scene 1

The English camp at Agincourt. Enter the **King, Gloucester** *and* **Bedford.**

King Henry   Gloucester, 'tis true that we are in great
      danger;
   The greater therefore should our courage be.
   Good morrow, brother Bedford. God Almighty!
5 There is some soul of goodness in things evil,
   Would men observingly distil it out –
   For our bad neighbour makes us early stirrers,
   Which is both healthful and good husbandry.
   Besides, they are our outward consciences,
10 And preachers to us all, admonishing
   That we should dress us fairly for our end.
   Thus may we gather honey from the weed
   And make a moral of the devil himself.

   [*Enter* **Sir Thomas Erpingham**]

   Good morrow, old Sir Thomas Erpingham.
15 A good soft pillow for that good white head
   Were better than a churlish turf of France.

Erpingham   Not so, my liege. This lodging likes me better,
   Since I may say, 'Now lie I like a king'.

King Henry   'Tis good for men to love their present pains
20 Upon example. So the spirit is eased,
   And when the mind is quickened, out of doubt
   The organs, though defunct and dead before,
   Break up their drowsy grave and newly move
   With casted slough and fresh legerity.
25 Lend me thy cloak, Sir Thomas. Brothers both,
   Commend me to the princes in our camp.
   Do my good-morrow to them, and anon
   Desire them all to my pavilion.

Scene 1

The English Camp. *Enter* **King Henry,** *the* **Duke of Gloucester,** *and the* **Duke of Bedford**.

King Henry   Gloucester, it's true we are in great danger: therefore our courage should be all the greater. Good morning, brother Bedford. God almighty! All evil has a trace of good in it, if only men would search it out: our disagreeable neighbours have made us rise early, which is both healthy and efficient. Besides, they are our outer consciences and our priests, counselling us to prepare ourselves properly for our end. Thus we can, as they say, 'gather honey from the weed', and draw a moral from the devil himself.

[**Sir Thomas Erpingham** *enters*]

Good morning, old Sir Thomas Erpingham. A good soft pillow for that good white head would be better than rough French turf!

Erpingham   Not so, my liege. This lodging suits me better, because I can say 'Now I sleep like a king'.

King Henry   [*aside*] It's good when men cherish their discomfort because of the example set by others. It encourages them, and when the mind is stimulated, there's no doubt that limbs that were previously inert and dead throw off their sluggishness, and begin to move again with renewed vigour and nimbleness. [*Aloud*] Lend me your cloak, Sir Thomas. [*To* **Gloucester** *and* **Bedford**] Brothers, give my regards to the princes in our camp; say good morning to them on my behalf, and ask them all to go to my tent.

159

Gloucester   We shall, my liege.

30   **Erpingham**   Shall I attend your grace?

King Henry   No, my good knight.
Go with my brothers to my lords of England.
I and my bosom must debate awhile,
And then I would no other company.

35   **Erpingham**   The Lord in heaven bless thee, noble Harry.

King Henry   God-a-mercy, old heart, thou speak'st
cheerfully.

[*Exeunt all but* **King Henry**]

[*Enter* **Pistol**]

Pistol   *Qui va là?*

King Henry   A friend.

40   **Pistol**   Discuss unto me: art thou officer?
Or art thou base, common, and popular?

King Henry   I am a gentleman of a company.

Pistol   Trail'st thou the puissant pike?

King Henry   Even so. What are you?

45   **Pistol**   As good a gentleman as the emperor.

King Henry   Then you are a better than the King.

Pistol   The King's a bawcock and a heart of gold,
A lad of life, an imp of fame,
Of parents good, of fist most valiant.
50   I kiss his dirty shoe, and from heartstring
I love the lovely bully. What is thy name?

King Henry   Harry Leroi.

Gloucester   We shall, my liege.

Erpingham   Shall I stay with your grace?

King Henry   No, my good knight. Go with my brothers to the nobles of England. I must think some things out, and need to be alone.

Erpingham   The Lord in heaven bless you, noble Harry!

King Henry   God bless you, old heart, you speak cheerfully!

[**Gloucester, Bedford** *and* **Sir Thomas** *leave.* **Pistol** *enters*]

Pistol   Who goes there?

King Henry   A friend.

Pistol   Reveal yourself: are you an officer? Or are you one of the common herd?

King Henry   No, sir, I am a freelance volunteer.

Pistol   Are you a wielder of the powerful pike? [*A pike could be up to 20 feet long*]

King Henry   Precisely. What are you?

Pistol   As good a gentleman as the Holy Roman Emperor.

King Henry   Then you are superior to the King?

Pistol   The King's a fine fellow, a good sport; a lively lad; one of the boys; comes from a good family; can use his fists. I kiss his dirty shoe! With all my heart, I love the lovely laddie! What is your name?

King Henry   Harry Leroy. [*'le roi' = the king*]

161

Pistol   Leroi? A Cornish name. Art thou of Cornish crew?

King Henry   No, I am a Welshman.

55 **Pistol**   Know'st thou Fluellen?

King Henry   Yes.

Pistol   Tell him I'll knock his leek about his pate
Upon Saint Davy's day.

King Henry   Do not you wear your dagger in your cap
60   that day, lest he knock that about yours.

Pistol   Art thou his friend?

King Henry   And his kinsman too.

Pistol   The figo for thee then!

King Henry   I thank you. God be with you.

65 **Pistol**   My name is Pistol called.

King Henry   It sorts well with your fierceness.

[*Exit* **Pistol**]

[*Enter* **Fluellen** *and* **Gower**]

Gower   Captain Fluellen!

Fluellen   So! In the name of Jesu Christ, speak lower. It is
the greatest admiration in the universal world, when the
70   true and ancient prerogatifs and laws of the wars is not
kept. If you would take the pains but to examine the
wars of Pompey the Great, you shall find, I warrant
you, that there is no tiddle-taddle nor pibble-babble in
Pompey's camp. I warrant you, you shall find the

Pistol   Leroy? A Cornish name. Are you one of the
Cornish lot?

King Henry   No. I'm a Welshman.

Pistol   Do you know Fluellen?

King Henry   Yes.

Pistol   Tell him I'll hit him over the head with his leek
upon St David's day! [*St David is the patron saint of
Wales, honoured on March 1st*]

King Henry   You'd better not wear your dagger in
your cap that day, in case he hits you with that.

Pistol   Are you his friend?

King Henry   And a relative, too.

Pistol   [*with a rude gesture*] Up yours.

King Henry   Thank you. God be with you.

Pistol   My name is Pistol.

King Henry   It suits your fierceness . . .

[**Pistol** *swaggers off.* **Fluellen** *and* **Gower** *enter.* **King
Henry** *listens at a distance*]

Gower   Captain Fluellen!

Fluellen   Indeed so. In the name of Jesus Christ,
speak lower! It is the most astonishing thing in the
whole wide world when the correct and ancient
rights and rules of war are not kept. If you would
just take the trouble to examine the wars of Pompey
the Great, you will find, I assure you, that there was
no chitter-chatter or nitter-natter in Pompey's camp!
I assure you that you'll find the procedures of war,

75   ceremonies of the wars, and the cares of it, and the
        forms of it, and the sobriety of it, and the modesty of it,
        to be otherwise.

Gower   Why, the enemy is loud. You hear him all night.

Fluellen   If the enemy is an ass and a fool and a prating
80   coxcomb, is it meet, think you, that we should also, look
        you, be an ass and a fool and a prating coxcomb? In
        your own conscience now?

Gower   I will speak lower.

Fluellen   I pray you and beseech you that you will.

                    [*Exeunt* **Fluellen** *and* **Gower**]

85 **King Henry**   Though it appear a little out of fashion,
        There is much care and valour in this Welshman.

        [*Enter three soldiers:* **John Bates, Alexander Court,** *and*
        Michael Williams]

Court   Brother John Bates, is not that the morning which
        breaks yonder?

Bates   I think it be. But we have no great cause to desire
90   the approach of day.

Williams   We see yonder the beginning of the day, but I
        think we shall never see the end of it. Who goes there?

King Henry   A friend.

Williams   Under what captain serve you?

95 **King Henry**   Under Sir Thomas Erpingham.

Williams   A good old commander and a most kind
        gentleman. I pray you, what thinks he of our estate?

and the concerns of it, and the good order of it, and the seriousness of it, and the self-control of it, to be otherwise!

Gower   Why, the enemy is noisy. You can hear him all night.

Fluellen   If the enemy is an ass and a fool and a jibbering idiot, is it wise, do you think, that we should also, look you, be an ass and a fool and a jibbering idiot? In all honesty, now?

Gower   [*resigned*] I will speak lower . . .

Fluellen   I beg and pray that you will.

[**Fluellen** *and* **Gower** *leave*]

King Henry   There's a great deal of commitment and valour in this Welshman, though it seems rather out-of-date.

[*Three soldiers enter:* **John Bates, Alexander Court,** *and* **Michael Williams**]

Court   Brother John Bates: isn't that morning breaking over yonder?

Bates   I think it is. We've no great reason to long for daybreak.

Williams   We see yonder the beginning of the day, but I think we'll never see the end of it. [*Seeing* **King Henry**] Who goes there?

King Henry   A friend.

Williams   Which captain do you serve under?

King Henry   Under Sir Thomas Erpingham.

Williams   A good old commander and a very kind gentleman. Tell me, how does he rate our chances?

165

King Henry   Even as men wrecked upon a sand, that look
to be washed off the next tide.

100 **Bates**   He hath not told his thought to the King?

King Henry   No, nor it is not meet he should. For though
I speak it to you, I think the King is but a man, as I
am. The violet smells to him as it doth to me; the
element shows to him as it doth to me. All his senses
105 have but human conditions. His ceremonies laid by, in
his nakedness he appears but a man, and though his
affections are higher mounted than ours, yet when they
stoop, they stoop with the like wing. Therefore, when he
sees reason of fears, as we do, his fears, out of doubt, be
110 of the same relish as ours are. Yet, in reason, no man
should possess him with any appearance of fear, lest he,
by showing it, should dishearten his army.

Bates   He may show what outward courage he will, but I
believe, as cold a night as 'tis, he could wish himself in
115 Thames up to the neck. And so I would he were, and I
by him, at all adventures, so we were quit here.

King Henry   By my troth, I will speak my conscience of
the King. I think he would not wish himself anywhere
but where he is.

120 **Bates**   Then I would he were here alone. So should he be
sure to be ransomed, and a many poor men's lives
saved.

King Henry   I dare say you love him not so ill to wish him
here alone, howsoever you speak this to feel other men's
125 minds. Methinks I could not die anywhere so contented
as in the King's company, his cause being just and his
quarrel honourable.

King Henry   Rather as if we were wrecked on a sandbank, and expected to be washed off by the next tide.

Bates   He hasn't said that to the King?

King Henry   No, nor is it proper that he should. Though I say it myself, I think the King is only a man, like I am. The violet smells the same to him as it does to me. The sky looks the same to him as it does to me. All his senses have human limitations. Take away his robes, and naked he's just like any other man, and though his ambitions are loftier than ours, when they plummet, they come down to earth just the same. Therefore, when he sees reason for fear, like we do, his fears, beyond all doubt, are just like ours. Still, it's commonsense that nobody should frighten the King by looking scared, in case the King shows it too and his army is disheartened.

Bates   He can show whatever outward courage he likes, but I believe, cold as this night is, he'd prefer to be up to his neck in the Thames. And I wish he was, too, and me with him at all events, so we were out of this place.

King Henry   Really. I'm quite certain how the King feels. I think he wouldn't wish himself anywhere other than he is.

Bates   Then I wish he were here alone. Then he'd be certain to be ransomed, and many poor men's lives would be saved.

King Henry   I'll bet you don't dislike him that much, to wish him here alone, however much you say it to test what other men think. Personally, I couldn't die anywhere so contented as in the King's company, his cause being just and his dispute honourable.

Williams   That's more than we know.

Bates   Ay, or more than we should seek after. For we
130   know enough if we know we are the King's subjects. If
his cause be wrong, our obedience to the King wipes the
crime of it out of us.

Williams   But if the cause be not good, the King himself
hath a heavy reckoning to make, when all those legs and
135   arms and heads chopped off in a battle shall join
together at the latter day, and cry all, 'We died at such
a place', some swearing, some crying for a surgeon,
some upon their wives left poor behind them, some upon
the debts they owe, some upon their children rawly left. I
140   am afeard there are few die well that die in a battle, for
how can they charitably dispose of anything, when blood
is their argument? Now, if these men do not die well, it
will be a black matter for the King that led them to it –
who to disobey were against all proportion of subjection.

145 **King Henry**   So, if a son that is by his father sent about
merchandise do sinfully miscarry upon the sea, the
imputation of his wickedness, by your rule, should be
imposed upon his father, that sent him. Or if a servant,
under his master's command transporting a sum of
150   money, be assailed by robbers, and die in many
irreconciled iniquities, you may call the business of the
master the author of the servant's damnation. But this is
not so. The King is not bound to answer the particular
endings of his soldiers, the father of his son, nor the
155   master of his servant, for they purpose not their death
when they purpose their services. Besides, there is no

Williams   That's more than we know.

Bates   Ay, or more than we should want to know. We know enough if we know we are the King's subjects. If his cause is a wrong one, our duty of obedience to the King wipes the crime of it out of us.

Williams   But if the cause isn't a good one, the King himself has a lot on his conscience when all those legs and arms and heads chopped off in battle join together on the Day of Judgement, and all cry 'We died at such a place': some cursing; some crying for a surgeon; some worrying about their wives left poor behind them; some about the debts they owe; some about their children left unprovided for. I'm afraid there are few die well that die in a battle, 'cos how can they express any Christian charity when killing is their business? Now if these men do not die well, it will be a very serious matter for the King who led them into it, and whom no subject can properly disobey.

King Henry   So, if a son, sent on business by his father, should die in a state of sin while at sea, by your rule the responsibility for his wickedness should lie with his father, who sent him. Or, if a servant carrying a sum of money on his master's orders should be attacked by robbers and die without confessing his sins, you could say that the master's business was the cause of the servant's damnation. But this is not so. The King is not answerable for the individual deaths of his soldiers, nor the father for his son's, nor the master for his servant's because they did not intend them to die when they sought their services. Besides, there is

169

King, be his cause never so spotless, if it come to the
arbitrement of swords, can try it out with all unspotted
soldiers. Some, peradventure, have on them the guilt of
160   premeditated and contrived murder; some, of beguiling
virgins with the broken seals of perjury; some, making
the wars their bulwark, that have before gored the gentle
bosom of peace with pillage and robbery. Now, if these
men have defeated the law and outrun native
165   punishment, though they can outstrip men, they have no
wings to fly from God. War is his beadle. War is his
vengeance. So that here men are punished for before-
breach of the King's laws, in now the King's quarrel.
Where they feared the death, they have borne life away;
170   and where they would be safe, they perish. Then if they
die unprovided, no more is the King guilty of their
damnation than he was before guilty of those impieties
for the which they are now visited. Every subject's duty
is the King's, but every subject's soul is his own.
175   Therefore should every soldier in the wars do as every
sick man in his bed: wash every mote out of his
conscience. And dying so, death is to him advantage; or
not dying, the time was blessedly lost wherein such
preparation was gained. And in him that escapes, it
180   were not sin to think that, making God so free an offer,
he let him outlive that day to see his greatness and to
teach others how they should prepare.

    Williams   'Tis certain, every man that dies ill, the ill upon
his own head. The King is not to answer it.

185 **Bates**   I do not desire he should answer for me, and yet I
determine to fight lustily for him.

no king – however spotless his cause – who could fight with none but spotless soldiers, if it came to a battle. Some undoubtedly would be guilty of premeditated murder, some of seducing virgins with broken promises, some, who have previously broken the peace with pillage and robbery, of using wars to give them protection. Now, if these men have defeated the law and escaped their rightful punishment, though they can run away from man, they've no means of fleeing from God. War is God's warrant officer. War is his vengeance. So that men are punished for previous breaches of the King's laws, in the battle that is now the King's business. Where they feared hanging, they took life away; where they seek safety, they perish. So if they die unprepared, the King is no more guilty of their damnation than he was earlier guilty of their crimes. Every subject's duty is to the King, but every subject's soul is his own. Therefore every soldier in war should do the same as every sick man in his bed: he should cleanse his conscience of every sin; however small. Dying that way, death is an advantage to him. Should he not die, the time lost in making the preparations was blessed. And in the case of the man who escapes with his life, it would not be sinful to think that, having made God so complete a confession, God allowed him to survive that day: to have his greatness revealed, and to teach others how they should prepare for death.

Williams   Every man who dies in sin, it's on his own head, that's for sure. The King isn't responsible.

Bates   I don't expect the King to answer for me – yet I'm determined to fight as hard as I can for him.

King Henry   I myself heard the King say he would not be
ransomed.

190 **Williams**   Ay, he said so, to make us fight cheerfully, but
when our throats are cut he may be ransomed, and we
ne'er the wiser.

King Henry   If I live to see it, I will never trust his word
after.

195 **Williams**   You pay him then! That's a perilous shot out of
an elder-gun, that a poor and private displeasure can do
against a monarch. You may as well go about to turn
the sun to ice with fanning in his face with a peacock's
feather. You'll never trust his word after! Come, 'tis a
foolish saying.

200 **King Henry**   Your reproof is something too round. I should
be angry with you, if the time were convenient.

Williams   Let it be a quarrel between us, if you live.

King Henry   I embrace it.

Williams   How shall I know thee again?

205 **King Henry**   Give me any gage of thine, and I will wear it
in my bonnet. Then if ever thou darest acknowledge it, I
will make it my quarrel.

Williams   Here's my glove. Give me another of thine.

King Henry   There.

[*They exchange gloves*]

210 **Williams**   This will I also wear in my cap. If ever thou
come to me and say, after tomorrow, 'This is my glove',
by this hand I will take thee a box on the ear.

King Henry I myself heard the King say he would not allow himself to be taken prisoner and ransomed.

Williams Yes, he said that to make us fight cheerfully, but when our throats are cut he may be ransomed and we won't be any the wiser.

King Henry If I live to see that happen, I'll never trust his word again.

Williams You tick him off then! That's a fearsome bullet to fire from a pop-gun: your personal disapproval versus a monarch! You might as well try turning the sun to ice by fanning it with a peacock's feather! 'You'll never trust his word again!' Come now: that's a ridiculous thing to say!

King Henry Your retort is somewhat too tactless. I'd be angry with you if the time was right.

Williams Let it be a quarrel between us, if you survive.

King Henry I accept the challenge.

Williams How will I recognise you again?

King Henry Give me some token of yours, and I'll wear it in my cap. Then if you ever dare to acknowledge it, I'll take up the quarrel.

Williams Here's my glove. Give me one of yours.

King Henry There.

[*They exchange gloves*]

Williams I'll wear this one in my cap, too. If ever you come to me and say, after tomorrow, 'This is my glove', by this hand – I'll box your ears!

King Henry   If ever I live to see it, I will challenge it.

Williams   Thou darest as well be hanged.

215 **King Henry**   Well, I will do it, though I take thee in the
King's company.

Williams   Keep thy word. Fare thee well.

Bates   Be friends, you English fools, be friends. We have
French quarrels enough, if you could tell how to reckon.

220 **King Henry**   Indeed, the French may lay twenty French
crowns to one they will beat us, for they bear them on
their shoulders. But it is no English treason to cut
French crowns, and tomorrow the King himself will be a
clipper.

[Exeunt soldier

225   Upon the King! Let us our lives, our souls
Our debts, our careful wives,
Our children, and our sins, lay on the King.
We must bear all. Oh hard condition,
Twin-born with greatness: subject to the breath
230   Of every fool, whose sense no more can feel
But his own wringing! What infinite heartsease
Must kings neglect that private men enjoy?
And what have kings that privates have not too,
Save ceremony, save general ceremony?
235   And what art thou, thou idol ceremony?
What kind of god art thou, that suffer'st more
Of mortal griefs than do thy worshippers?
What are thy rents? What are thy comings-in?
Oh ceremony, show me but thy worth.
240   What is thy soul of adoration?

King Henry   If I should live to see it, I will challenge it.

Williams   You'd dare as well be hanged!

King Henry   Well, I'll do it, even if it is in the presence of the King.

Williams   Keep your word! Fare you well.

Bates   Be friends, you English fools, be friends! We have enough quarrels with the French, if you could count!

King Henry   Indeed, the French could lay 20-1 that they'll beat us, they've so many crowns on their shoulders. [*'Crowns' were French gold coins as well as men's heads*] It's not illegal for an Englishman to cut them down [*it was against the law to reduce the size of English coinage*], and tomorrow the King himself will be doing some clipping . . .

[*The soldiers leave*]

The King responsible!

'Let us make our lives, our souls, our debts, our worried wives, our children, and our sins the responsibility of the King'. We must shoulder everything. Such an onerous burden. Oh, harsh affliction! Inseparable from royalty: to be subject to the grouses of every self-centred fool. What infinite serenity are kings denied that those in private life enjoy? And what have kings that laymen don't have too, except ceremony, universal ceremony? And what are you, you idol known as 'ceremony'? What kind of god are you, to suffer more of mortal griefs than any of your worshippers? What are your rewards? What are your revenues? Oh, ceremony, show me your advantages! What is at the heart of

175

Art thou aught else but place, degree, and form,
Creating awe and fear in other men?
Wherein thou art less happy, being feared,
Than they in fearing.
245 What drink'st thou oft, instead of homage sweet,
But poisoned flattery? Oh be sick, great greatness,
And bid thy ceremony give thee cure!
Think'st thou the fiery fever will go out
With titles blown from adulation?
250 Will it give place to flexure and low bending?
Canst thou, when thou command'st the beggar's knee,
Command the health of it? No, thou proud dream
That play'st so subtly with a king's repose;
I am a king that find thee, and I know
255 'Tis not the balm, the sceptre, and the ball,
The sword, the mace, the crown imperial,
The intertissued robes of gold and pearl,
The farced title running 'fore the king,
The throne he sits on, nor the tide of pomp
260 That beats upon the high shore of this world –
No, not all these, thrice-gorgeous ceremony,
Not all these, laid in bed majestical,
Can sleep so soundly as the wretched slave
Who with a body filled and vacant mind
265 Gets him to rest, crammed with distressful bread;
Never sees horrid night, the child of hell,
But like a lackey from the rise to set
Sweats in the eye of Phoebus, and all night
Sleeps in Elysium; next day, after dawn
270 Doth rise and help Hyperion to his horse,
And follows so the ever-running year
With profitable labour to his grave.
And, but for ceremony, such a wretch,
Winding up days with toil and nights with sleep,
275 Had the forehand and vantage of a king.

176

our worshipping you? Are you nothing more than social rank and ritual, creating awe and fear in other men? In which respect the king is less happy in being feared than those who fear him are. Instead of sweet respect, isn't poisoned flattery what he mostly gets? Oh, just be ill, great high and mighty one, and order ceremony to cure you! Do you suppose your raging fever will subside if fanned by the flatteries of those who fawn upon you? Will it yield to bowing and scraping? When you make the beggar bend his knee, can you also influence the health of it? No, ceremony, you vain illusion that so subtly plays upon a monarch's peace of mind. I am a King and I expose you. I know it's not the consecrated oil, the royal sceptre, the orb of sovereignty, the sword, the mace, the crown imperial, the robes of interwoven gold and pearl, the fancy royal titles, the throne he sits on, nor the omnipresent pomp that surrounds the mighty, no not all these, most gorgeous ceremony, not all these reposing on a royal bed can sleep as soundly as the wretched slave. With a tired body and a carefree mind, he goes to sleep, his stomach crammed with the coarsest bread. He never wakens in the horrid, hell-like blackness of night, but like the sun god's footmen, he sweats from dawn till dusk and all night sleeps in bliss. Next day, after dawn, he rises to help his master ride his horse, and goes through all the years of his life with purposeful labour to his grave. And ceremony apart, such a wretch – filling his days with toil and his nights with sleep – has the advantage over a king. The serf – a

The slave, a member of the country's peace,
Enjoys it, but in gross brain little wots
What watch the King keeps to maintain the peace,
Whose hours the peasant best advantages.

[*Enter* **Erpingham**]

280 **Erpingham**   My lord, your nobles, jealous of your absence,
Seek through the camp to find you.

King Henry   Good old knight
Collect them all together at my tent.
I'll be there before thee.

285 **Erpingham**   I shall do't, my lord

[*Exit*

King Henry   Oh God of battles! steel my soldiers' hearts,
Possess them not with fear. Take from them now
The sense of reck'ning, ere th'opposed numbers
Pluck their hearts from them. Not today, oh Lord,
290 Oh not today, think not upon the fault
My father made in compassing the crown.
I Richard's body have interred new,
And on it have bestowed more contrite tears
Than from it issued forced drops of blood.
295 Five hundred poor I have in yearly pay
Who twice a day their withered hands hold up
Toward heaven to pardon blood. And I have built
Two chantries, where the sad and solemn priests
Sing still for Richard's soul. More will I do,
300 Though all that I can do is nothing worth,
Since that my penitence comes after all,
Imploring pardon.

[*Enter* **Gloucester**]

Gloucester   My liege.

member of the orderly realm — enjoys the benefits
of peace; but with his dull brain he little realises
how vigilant the King must be to maintain that
peace, the peasant profiting most from his labours.

[**Sir Thomas Erpingham** *enters*]

Erpingham   My lord, your nobles, anxious about your
absence, are searching the camp to find you.

King Henry   Good old knight, collect them all together
at my tent. I'll be there before you.

Erpingham   I'll do that, my lord.

[*He goes*]

King Henry   Oh God of battles, steel my soldiers'
hearts. Do not make them afraid. Take from them
now their ability to count, in case the size of the
opposing army makes them scared. Not today, oh
lord, oh not today, do not think about my father's
misdeed in procuring the crown. [*He deposed
Richard II and became Henry IV*] I have re-interred
Richard's body [*in Westminster Abbey*] and I have
bestowed more remorseful tears on it than it ever
shed drops of murdered blood. I have given
annuities to five hundred poor, and twice a day they
raise their withered hands in prayer, beseeching
pardon. And I have built two chapels, where the
grave and solemn priests still sing for Richard's
soul. I will do more; though all I can do is
worthless, since my penitence and plea for pardon
come after all my gains . . .

[*The* **Duke of Gloucester** *enters*]

Gloucester   My liege . . .

King Henry   My brother Gloucester's voice? Ay
305   I know thy errand, I will go with thee.
     The day, my friends, and all things stay for me.

[Exeunt

Scene 2

The French Camp. Enter the **Dauphin, Orleans, Rambures**
and others.

Orleans   The sun doth gild our armour. Up, my lords!

Dauphin   *Montez à cheval*! My horse! Varlet, *lacquais*! Ha!

Orleans   Oh brave spirit!

Dauphin   *Via! Les eaux et la terre!*

5 **Orleans**   *Rien plus? L'air et le feu!*

Dauphin   *Ciel*, cousin Orleans!

   [*Enter the* **Constable**]

   Now, my Lord Constable!

Constable   Hark how our steeds for present service neigh.

Dauphin   Mount them and make incision in their hides,
10   That their hot blood may spin in English eyes
     And doubt them with superfluous courage. Ha!

Rambures   What, will you have them weep our horses'
     blood?
     How shall we then behold their natural tears?

   [*Enter a* **Messenger**]

King Henry   My brother Gloucester's voice? Yes. I
know your errand. I'll go with you. The day, my
friends, and everything are waiting for me.

[*They go*]

Scene 2

The French Camp. Enter the **Dauphin**, *the* **Dukes of
Bourbon** *and* **Orleans**, *and* **Lord Rambures**

Orleans   The sun gilds our armour. Up, my lords!

Dauphin   To the saddle! My horse! My equerry, there!

Orleans   Oh, brave spirit!

Dauphin   Over earth and through water!

Orleans   Is that all? Air and fire!

Dauphin   The heavens, cousin Orleans!

[**The Constable of France** *enters*]

Now, my Lord Constable!

Constable   Listen to our horses neighing for action.

Dauphin   Mount them, and bleed them with your
spurs to cool their ardour – so their hot blood will
spurt into English eyes and daub them with a show
of courage.

Rambures   What, will you have them weeping our
horses' blood? How then shall we see their natural
tears?

[A **Messenger** *enters*]

15 **Messenger**   The English are embattled, you French peers.

Constable   To horse, you gallant princes, straight to
      horse!
Do but behold yon poor and starved band,
And your fair show shall suck away their souls,
20 Leaving them but the shells and husks of men.
There is not work enough for all our hands;
Scarce blood enough in all their sickly veins
To give each naked curtal-axe a stain;
That our French gallants shall today draw out
25 And sheathe for lack of sport. Let us but blow on them,
The vapour of our valour will o'erturn them.
'Tis positive 'gainst all exceptions, lords,
That our superfluous lackeys and our peasants,
Who in unnecessary action swarm
30 About our squares of battle, were enow
To purge this field of such a hilding foe,
Though we upon this mountain's basis by
Took stand for idle speculation,
But that our honours must not. What's to say?
35 A very little little let us do
And all is done. Then let the trumpets sound
The tucket sonance and the note to mount,
For our approach shall so much dare the field
That England shall couch down in fear and yield.

      [*Enter* **Grandpré**]

40 **Grandpré**   Why do you stay so long, my lords of France?
Yon island carrions, desperate of their bones,
Ill-favouredly become the morning field.
Their ragged curtains poorly are let loose
And our air shakes them passing scornfully.
45 Big Mars seems bankrupt in their beggared host
And faintly through a rusty beaver peeps.

Messenger   The English are lined up for battle,
gentlemen.

Constable   To your horses, gallant princes!
Straightway to your horses! Just take a look at that
poor and starving army there, and your fine
splendour will drain them of their souls, leaving
them just the shells and husks of men. There isn't
enough work for all of us; hardly enough blood in
all their sickly veins to stain every cutlass that is
out; so our French lads will be drawing their swords
and sheathing them again for want of sport. If we
just blow on them, our valorous breath will knock
them over. Beyond all doubt, my lords, our menials
and our peasants, who clutter around our fighting
men, would be sufficient to clear this battlefield of
such a contemptible foe, even if we just stood here
on these foothills and watched out of idle curiosity:
except that our honour wouldn't let us do it. What
more can be said? Let us do the absolute minimum,
and we've won. Then let the trumpets sound, the
fanfares blow, and the notes ring out – for our
advance will so benumb the enemy that King Henry
will crouch down in fear and surrender.

[**Lord Grandpré** *enters*]

Grandpré   Why do you delay so long, my lords of
France? Those island corpses, indifferent to their
safety, are making the morning field look untidy.
Their tattered banners droop in misery, and our air
makes them shudder as it scornfully passes them
by. Great Mars, the god of war, looks shabby as
he's represented by their tatty army, and feebly

The horsemen sit like fixed candlesticks
With torchstaves in their hands, and their poor jades
Lob down their heads, drooping the hides and hips,
50   The gum down-roping from their pale dead eyes,
And in their palled dull mouths the gimmaled bit
Lies foul with chawed grass, still and motionless,
And their executors, the knavish crows,
Fly o'er them, all impatient for their hour.
55   Description cannot suit itself in words
To demonstrate the life of such a battle
In life so lifeless as it shows itself.

Constable   They have said their prayers, and they stay for
death.

60   **Dauphin**   Shall we go send them dinners and fresh suits
And give their fasting horses provender,
And after fight with them?

Constable   I stay but for my guidon. To the field!
I will the banner from a trumpet take
65   And use it for my haste. Come, come away!
The sun is high, and we outwear the day.

[*Exeunt*]

Scene 3

The English camp. Enter **Gloucester, Bedford, Exeter,
Salisbury, Warwick** *and* **Erpingham,** *with all the host.*

Gloucester   Where is the King?

Bedford   The King himself is rode to view their battle.

peeps out through a rusty visor. The cavalry sit like ornamental candlesticks with torches in their hands. Their poor nags hang their heads, sagging in the middle, mucus drooling from their lack-lustre eyes; and in their weak, pale mouths the gimmal-bit lies befouled with chewed grass, still and motionless. Their undertakers, the unscrupulous crows, fly above them, all impatient for their time to come. There are no adequate words to describe such an army, when it consists of the living dead as this one does.

Constable They have said their prayers, and await their deaths.

Dauphin Shall we send them dinners and fresh clothes, and give their starving horses provender, and then fight with them afterwards?

Constable All I need now is my pennant. To the field! I'll take a banner from a trumpeter and use that instead, to save time. Come, come away! The sun has risen high, and we are wasting time!

[*They leave for the battlefield*]

Scene 3

The battlefield. The **Dukes of Gloucester, Bedford** *and* **Exeter**, *the* **Earls of Salisbury** *and* **Warwick, Sir Thomas Erpingham**, *and the English Army are ready to face the French.*

Gloucester Where is the King?

Bedford The King has ridden to view their army personally.

185

Warwick   Of fighting men they have full threescore
thousand.

5 **Exeter**   There's five to one. Besides, they all are fresh.

Salisbury   God's arm strike with us! 'Tis a fearful odds.
God b'you, princes all. I'll to my charge.
If we no more meet till we meet in heaven,
Then joyfully, my noble Lord of Bedford,
10 My dear Lord Gloucester, and my good Lord Exeter,
And [*to* **Warwick**] my kind kinsman: warriors all, adieu!

Bedford   Farewell, good Salisbury, and good luck go with
thee!

Exeter   Farewell, kind lord. Fight valiantly today –
15 And yet I do thee wrong to mind thee of it,
For thou art framed of the firm truth of valour.

[*Exit* **Salisbury**]

Bedford   He is as full of valour as of kindness,
Princely in both.

[*Enter* **King Henry**]

Westmorland   Oh that we now had here
20 But one ten thousand of those men in England
That do no work today!

King Henry   What's he that wishes so?
My cousin Westmorland? No, my fair cousin.
If we are marked to die, we are enow
25 To do our country loss; and if to live,
The fewer men, the greater share of honour.
God's will, I pray thee wish not one man more.
By Jove, I am not covetous for gold,
Nor care I who doth feed upon my cost;
30 It ernes me not if men my garments wear;
Such outward things dwell not in my desires.

Warwick   They have fully 60,000 fighting men.

Exeter   That's five to one. Besides, they are all fresh.

Salisbury   May God be on our side! These are fearful odds. God be with you, princes all. I'll take up my command. If we do not meet again till we meet in heaven, then joyfully, my noble Lord of Bedford, my dear Lord Gloucester, my good Lord Exter, and [*to the* **Earl of Warwick**] my kind kinsman — warriors all — goodbye!

Bedford   Farewell, good Salisbury and good luck go with you.

Exeter   Farewell, kind lord. Fight bravely today: and yet I do you an injustice to remind you of it, since you are the essence of valour.

[**Salisbury** *goes*]

Bedford   He is as brave as he is kind, princely in both.

[**King Henry** *enters, unseen by the others at first*]

Westmorland   Oh, if only we had here now just one ten thousand of those in England who have no work today!

[**The King** *comes forward*]

King Henry   Who wishes that? My cousin Westmorland? No, good cousin. If we are marked down to die, we are enough for our country to lose; and if to live, the fewer men the greater the share of honour. In God's name, do not wish for one more man. I swear I don't want gold; nor do I care who eats at my expense; I'm not concerned who wears my clothes. Such outward things form no part of

But if it be a sin to covet honour
I am the most offending soul alive.
No, faith, my coz, wish not a man from England.
35 God's peace, I would not lose so great an honour
As one man more methinks would share from me
For the best hope I have. Oh do not wish one more.
Rather proclaim it, Westmorland, through my host
That he which hath no stomach to this fight,
40 Let him depart. His passport shall be made
And crowns for convoy put into his purse.
We would not die in that man's company
That fears his fellowship to die with us.
This day is called the Feast of Crispian.
45 He that outlives this day and comes safe home
Will stand a-tiptoe when this day is named
And rouse him at the name of Crispian.
He that shall live this day and see old age
Will yearly on the vigil feast his neighbours
50 And say, 'Tomorrow is Saint Crispian'.
Then will he strip his sleeve and show his scars
And say, 'These wounds I had on Crispin's day'.
Old men forget; yet all shall be forgot,
But he'll remember, with advantages,
55 What feats he did that day. Then shall our names,
Familiar in his mouth as household words –
Harry the King, Bedford and Exeter,
Warwick and Talbot, Salisbury and Gloucester –
Be in their flowing cups freshly remembered.
60 This story shall the good man teach his son,
And Crispin Crispian shall ne're go by
From this day to the ending of the world
But we in it shall be remembered,
We few, we happy few, we band of brothers;

my ambitions. But if it is a sin to covet honour, I am
the most offending man alive. No, indeed, cousin:
don't wish another man from England. God's peace,
I would not lose so great a share of the honour I
aspire to, as one man more would take from me.
No, don't ask for one more! Rather announce to my
army that anyone lacking the stomach for this fight
should leave us now. He'll be given a safe conduct,
and money for his travel put in his purse. We do
not wish to die in any man's company who lacks
the comradeship to die with us. This day is called
the Feast of Crispian [*October 25th*]. The man who
outlives this day and comes home safe will rally
when this day is named, and perk up at the name of
Crispian. The man who survives this day to reach
old age will feast his neighbours on the anniversary,
and say 'Tomorrow is Saint Crispian'. Then he will
roll his sleeve, and show his scars, and say 'I got
these wounds on Crispin's day'. Old men forget; but
though he remembers nothing else, he'll remember
– with embellishments! – what feats he did that
day. Then shall our names, as familiar to him as
household words – Harry the King, Bedford and
Exeter, Warwick and Talbot, Salisbury and
Gloucester – be remembered in their toasts. This
story the good man will teach his son, and Crispin
Crispian will never pass by from this day till the
ending of the world without our being remembered.

65   For he today that sheds his blood with me
      Shall be my brother; be he ne'er so vile,
      This day shall gentle his condition.
      And gentlemen in England now abed
      Shall think themselves accursed they were not here,
70   And hold their manhoods cheap whiles any speaks
      That fought with us upon Saint Crispin's day.

      [*Enter* **Salisbury**]

      Salisbury   My sovereign lord, bestow yourself with speed.
      The French are bravely in their battles set
      And will with all expedience charge on us.

75   **King Henry**   All things are ready if our minds be so.

      Warwick   Perish the man whose mind is backward now.

      King Henry   Thou dost not wish more help from England,
      coz?

      Warwick   God's will, my liege, would you and I alone,
80   Without more help, could fight this royal battle!

      King Henry   Why now thou hast unwished five thousand
          men,
      Which likes me better than to wish us one.
      You know your places. God be with you all.

      [*Tucket. Enter* **Montjoy**]

85   **Montjoy**   Once more I come to know of thee, King Harry,
      If for thy ransom thou wilt now compound
      Before thy most assured overthrow.
      For certainly thou art so near the gulf
      Thou needs must be englutted. Besides, in mercy

190

We few; we happy few; we band of brothers! The man who sheds his blood with me today shall be my brother; however humble he may be, this day will raise his stature. And gentlemen in England still lying in their beds will think themselves accursed because they were not here, and feel abashed when someone speaks who fought with us upon Saint Crispin's day!

[The **Earl of Salisbury** *enters*]

Salisbury   My sovereign lord, take up your position with all speed. The French are handsomely arrayed for battle, and they'll be charging us at any moment.

King Henry   Everything's ready if we're in the right frame of mind.

Warwick   Perish the man whose mind is still in doubt.

King Henry   You do not wish for extra help from England, cousin?

Warwick   By God, my liege, would that you and I alone, without more help, could fight this royal battle!

King Henry   Why, now you have unwished five thousand men! That suits me better than to wish an extra one! You know your places. God be with you all!

[*Fanfare.* **Montjoy** *the* **Herald** *appears*]

Montjoy   Once more I come to know from you, King Harry, whether you will negotiate your ransom before you are most assuredly defeated. You are so near the whirlpool you must be swallowed up by it.

90   The Constable desires thee thou wilt mind
     Thy followers of repentance, that their souls
     May make a peaceful and a sweet retire
     From off these fields where, wretches, their poor bodies
     Must lie and fester.

95   **King Henry**   Who hath sent thee now?

     Montjoy   The Constable of France.

     King Henry   I pray thee bear my former answer back.
     Bid them achieve me, and then sell my bones.
     Good God, why should they mock poor fellows thus?
100 The man that once did sell the lion's skin
     While the beast lived, was killed with hunting him.
     A many of our bodies shall no doubt
     Find native graves, upon the which, I trust,
     Shall witness live in brass of this day's work.
105 And those that leave their valiant bones in France,
     Dying like men, though buried in your dunghills
     They shall be famed. For there the sun shall greet them
     And draw their honours reeking up to heaven,
     Leaving their earthly parts to choke your clime,
110 The smell whereof shall breed a plague in France.
     Mark then abounding valour in our English,
     That, being dead, like to the bullet's grazing
     Break out into a second course of mischief,
     Killing in relapse of mortality.
115 Let me speak proudly. Tell the Constable
     We are but warriors for the working day.
     Our gayness and our gilt are all besmirched
     With rainy marching in the painful field.
     There's not a piece of feather in our host –
120 Good argument, I hope, we will not fly –
     And time hath worn us into slovenry.
     But, by the mass, our hearts are in the trim.

Besides, in his mercy, the Constable asks you to
make your followers mindful of repentance, so their
souls can depart peacefully and sweetly from these
fields where, wretches, their poor bodies must lie
and rot.

King Henry Who sent you this time?

Montjoy The Constable of France.

King Henry Take my former answer back. Let them
capture me first before they sell my bones. Good
God, why should they mock poor fellows like this?
The man [*in Aesop's fable*] who sold the lion's skin
while the beast was still alive, was killed while
hunting him. Many of our bodies will find graves at
home in England, on which, I trust, brass plaques
will be living witnesses of this day's work. And
those who leave their valiant bones in France, dying
like men they shall be revered, even if they are
buried in your dunghills. For there the sun will
shine on them, and draw out their honourable
souls; raising them up to heaven, and leaving their
bodies to foul your atmosphere, the smell of which
will breed a plague in France. Note the exceptional
valour of our English. Though dead, they're like a
ricochetting bullet; they start a second round of
destruction killing after they have been killed. Let
me speak proudly. Tell the Constable we are
professional soldiers. Our bright embroidered
clothes are all begrimed through marching in the
rain over difficult ground. There's not one
ornamental feather in our entire army – convincing
proof, I hope, that we won't fly away – and time has
made us all look slovenly. But by heaven, our hearts

And my poor soldiers tell me, yet ere night
They'll be in fresher robes, or they will pluck
125 The gay new coats o'er the French soldiers' heads,
And turn them out of service. If they do this –
As if God please, they shall – my ransom then
Will soon be levied. Herald, save thou thy labour.
Come thou no more for ransom, gentle herald.
130 They shall have none, I swear, but these my joints –
Which if they have as I will leave 'em them,
Shall yield them little. Tell the Constable.

   Montjoy   I shall, King Harry. And so fare thee well.
   Thou never shalt hear herald any more.

135 **King Henry**   I fear thou wilt once more come for a
   ransom.

[*Exit* **Montjoy**

[*Enter* **York**]

   York   My lord, most humbly on my knee I beg
   The leading of the vanguard.

   King Henry   Take it, brave York. Now soldiers, march
140   away,
   And how thou pleasest, God, dispose the day.

[*Exeunt*

are spic and span! And my poor soldiers tell me
that before tonight they'll all be wearing fresher
clothes; because they'll pull those bright new coats
over your French soldiers' heads, ending their
careers! If they do this – as they shall, God willing –
my ransom will then soon be paid. Herald, save
yourself some trouble. Don't come again for
ransom, gentle herald. The French will get nothing
but these limbs of mine, I swear to you; and in the
condition I shall leave them, they won't be worth a
lot. Tell the Constable that.

Montjoy   I shall, King Harry. And so, fare you well.
That's the last you'll hear from the herald.

King Henry   I suspect you'll come once more about a
ransom.

[**Montjoy** *leaves. The* **Duke of York** *enters*]

York   My lord, most humbly, and on my knees, I beg
the privilege of leading the vanguard.

King Henry   Take it, brave York. Now, soldiers,
march! God, Thy will be done today!

[*They proceed to battle*]

Scene 4

The field of battle. Alarum. Excusions. Enter **Pistol,** *a* **French Soldier,** *and the* **Boy.**

Pistol   Yield, cur.

French Soldier   *Je pense que vous êtes le gentilhomme de bon qualité.*

Pistol   Cality? 'Calin o custure me!'
5   Art thou a gentleman? What is thy name? Discuss.

French Soldier   *Oh, Seigneur Dieu!*

Pistol   [*aside*] Oh Seigneur Dew should be a gentleman.
       Perpend my words, oh Seigneur Dew, and mark:
       Oh Seigneur Dew, thou diest, on point of fox,
10   Except, oh Seigneur, thou do give to me
       Egregious ransom.

French Soldier   *Oh prenez miséricorde! Ayez pitié de moi!*

Pistol   'Moy' shall not serve; I will have forty 'moys'
       Or I will fetch thy rim out at thy throat
15   In drops of crimson blood.

French Soldier   *Est-il impossible d'échapper la force de ton bras?*

Pistol   Brass, cur? Thou damned and luxurious mountain
       goat.
20   Offer'st me brass?

Scene 4

*The field of battle. Soldiers of the French and English
armies fight their way across the stage. **Pistol** is under
pressure from a **Frenchman**, but the French soldier
slips and **Pistol** stands over him, the **Boy** at his side.
(NB As the humour in this scene cuts across two
languages, the spirit of it is conveyed in English only
throughout, and the French is not accurately
translated.)*

Pistol   Surrender, you dog!

French Soldier   I think you are a gentleman of noble
rank.

Pistol   Noble rank? [*He sings a snatch from an Irish
melody*] 'She was a noble maiden . . .' [*Back to
business again*] Are you a gentleman? What is your
name? Enlighten me!

French Soldier   Oh, Lord God!

Pistol   [*aside*] 'Lord God' sounds like a gentleman!
Harken to my words, Lord God, and take note. Lord
God, unless you give me gold in ransom, I'll have
your life!

French Soldier   Oh, mercy! An ounce of pity, please!

Pistol   An ounce isn't sufficient. I want forty, or else
I'll cut your bleeding throat.

French Soldier   Is it impossible to change a heart of
brass?

Pistol   Brass, cur? You damned, randy, mountain
goat. Do you dare to offer me brass?

French Soldier   *Oh pardonne-moi!*

Pistol   Sayest thou me so? Is that a ton of moys? –
Come hither boy. Ask me this slave in French
What is his name.

25 **Boy**   *Ecoutez: comment êtes-vous appelé?*

French Soldier   *Monsieur le Fer.*

Boy   He says his name is Master Fer.

Pistol   Master Fer? I'll fer him, and firk him, and ferret
him.
30 Discuss the same in French unto him.

Boy   I do not know the French for fer and ferret and firk.

Pistol   Bid him prepare, for I will cut his throat.

French Soldier   *Que dit-il, monsieur?*

Boy   *Il me commande à vous dire que vous faites vous prêt, car*
35 *ce soldat ici est disposé tout a cette heure de couper votre*
gorge.

Pistol   Owy, cuppele gorge, permafoy!
Peasant, unless thou give me crowns, brave crowns;
Or mangled shalt thou be by this my sword.

40 **French Soldier**   *Oh je vous supplie, pour l'amour de Dieu, me*
pardonner. Je suis gentilhomme de bonne maison. Gardez ma
vie, et je vous donnerai deux cents écus.

Pistol   What are his words?

Boy   He prays you to save his life. he is a gentleman of a
45 good house, and for his ransom he will give you two
hundred crowns.

Pistol   Tell him, my fury shall abate, and I
The crowns will take.

French Soldier   A thousand pardons!

Pistol   Did you say a thousand? Would that be a ton? Come here, boy. Ask this slave's name, in French.

Boy   Listen: what's your name?

French Soldier   Mr Iron.

Boy   He says his name is Mr Iron . . .

Pistol   Mr Iron? I'll iron him, and press him, and flatten him out! Convey this to him in French.

Boy   I don't know the French for 'to iron', or 'press', or 'flatten out'!

Pistol   Tell him to prepare himself. I shall cut his throat.

French Soldier   Sir, what did he say?

Boy   He told me to tell you to prepare yourself, because this soldier here is disposed to cut your throat right now.

Pistol   [*experimenting with French*] Ah, wee. Coo-pay your gorge, peasant, unless you give me money, good money. Otherwise my sword will chop you into pieces.

French Soldier   I beg you for the love of God, let me go. I am a gentleman from a good family. Save my life and I'll give you two hundred gold coins.

Pistol   What did he say?

Boy   He begs you to save his life. He is a gentleman of good family, and he'll give you two hundred gold coins as his ransom.

Pistol   Tell him: my fury shall subside. I'll take the cash.

French Soldier   *Petit monsieur, que dit-il?*

50   **Boy**   *Encore qu'il est contre son jurement de pardonner aucun
prisonnier, néanmoins, pour les écus que vous l'avez promis i,
est content à vous donner la liberté, le franchisement.*

French Soldier   [*kneeling to* **Pistol**] *Sur mes genoux je vous
donne mille remerciements, et je m'estime heureux que j'ai*
55   *tombé entre les mains d'un chevalier, je pense, le plus brave,
vaillant, et très distingué seigneur d'Angleterre.*

Pistol   Expound unto me, boy.

Boy   He gives you upon his knees a thousand thanks, and
he esteems himself happy that he hath fallen into the
60   hands of one, as he thinks, the most brave, valorous,
and thrice-worthy seigneur of England.

Pistol   As I suck blood, I will some mercy show.
Follow me.

Boy   *Suivez-vous le grand capitaine.*

[Exeunt **Pistol** *and* **French Soldier**

65   I did never know so full a voice issue from so empty a
heart. But the saying is true: 'the empty vessel makes the
greatest sound'. Bardolph and Nym had ten times more
valour than this roaring devil i'th'old play, that everyone
may pare his nails with a wooden dagger, and they are
70   both hanged, and so would this be, if he durst steal
anything adventurously. I must stay with the lackeys
with the luggage of our camp. The French might have a
good prey of us, if he knew of it, for there is none to
guard it but boys.

[Exit]

French Soldier   Little sir, what did he say?

Boy   Although it's against his better judgement to pardon any prisoner, nevertheless, in return for the gold you've promised him, he'll agree to give you your liberty, your freedom.

French Soldier   [*kneeling before* **Pistol**] On my knees I give you a thousand thanks, and count myself lucky to have fallen into the hands of a nobleman, I believe, who is the most brave, valiant, and thrice-worthy gentleman in all England!

Pistol   Translate, boy!

Boy   He gives you a thousand thanks, on his knees, and he feels fortunate that he has been captured by one of England's bravest, most courageous and thrice-worthy gentlemen.

Pistol   As I suck blood, I'll show some mercy! Follow me.

Boy   Follow the noble Captain!

[**Pistol** *and the* **French Soldier** *leave*]

I've never heard so much claptrap from so great a windbag! The saying is true: 'Empty vessels make the most sound'. Bardolph and Nym were ten times braver than this knockabout pantomime devil, and they've both been hanged. So would this one be, if he dared to steal anything! I must stay with the non-combatants who look after the army's tackle. The French could have easy pickings if they knew about it; the guards are only boys.

[*He goes*]

Scene 5

Another part of the field. Enter the **Constable, Orleans, Rambures, Bourbon** *and* **Dauphin.**

Constable   *Oh diable!*

Orleans   *Oh Seigneur! Le jour est perdu, tout est perdu!*

Dauphin   *Mort de ma vie!* All is confounded, all.
Reproach and everlasting shame
5   Sits mocking in our plumes

[*A short alarum*]

Oh *méchante* fortune! Do not run away.

Constable   Why, all our ranks are broke.

Dauphin   Oh, perdurable shame! Let's stab ourselves.
Be these the wretches that we played at dice for?

10 **Orleans**   Is this the king we sent to for his ransom?

Bourbon   Shame, and eternal shame, nothing but shame!
Let us die in honour. Once more back again,
And he that will not follow Bourbon now
Let him go hence, and with his cap in hand
15 Like a base pander, hold the chamber door
Whilst by a slave, no gentler than my dog,
His fairest daughter is contaminated.

Constable   Disorder, that hath spoiled us, friend us now!
Let us on heaps go offer up our lives.

20 **Orleans**   We are enow yet living in the field
To smother up the English in our throngs,
If any order might be thought upon.

Scene 5

On the French side of the battlefield. The **Constable of France**, *and the* **Dukes of Orleans** *and* **Bourbon**, *the* **Dauphin** *and* **Rambures** *enter in confusion and despair.*

Constable   Hell and damnation!

Orleans   Oh, your Highness! The day is lost, all is lost!

Dauphin   Oh, my God! We've lost everything: everything! Self-reproach and everlasting shame sit on our helmets, mocking us!

[*There is a short burst of hand-to-hand fighting*]

Such foul luck! [*To* **Rambures**] Do not run away!

Constable   We've broken ranks everywhere.

Dauphin   Oh, everlasting shame! Let's stab ourselves. Are these the wretches we played dice for?

Orleans   Is this the king we offered to ransom?

Bourbon   Shame, eternal shame! Nothing but shame! Let us die honourably. Once more – back again! The man who will not follow Bourbon now, may he depart, and holding out his cap like a contemptible pimp, guard the bedroom door whilst his fairest daughter is raped by a mongrel wretch.

Constable   May the chaos that has ruined us befriend us now! Let us sacrifice ourselves en masse!

Orleans   There's enough of us still living on the battlefield to smother the English by weight of numbers, if we had the right plan.

Bourbon   The devil take order now! I'll to the throng.
    Let life be short, else shame will be too long!

[Exeunt

Scene 6

Another part of the field. Alarum. Enter the **King** *and his
train, with prisoners.*

King Henry   Well have we done, thrice-valiant
    countrymen.
    But all's not done; yet keep the French the field.

Exeter   The Duke of York commends him to your majesty.

5 **King Henry**   Lives he, good uncle? Thrice within this hour
    I saw him down, thrice up again and fighting.
    From helmet to the spur, all blood he was.

Exeter   In which array, brave soldier, doth he lie,
    Larding the plain. And by his bloody side,
10   Yokefellow to his honour-owing wounds,
    The noble Earl of Suffolk also lies.
    Suffolk first died, and York, all haggled over,
    Comes to him, where in gore he lay insteeped,
    And takes him by the beard, kisses the gashes
15   That bloodily did yawn upon his face.
    He cries aloud, 'Tarry, my cousin Suffolk.
    My soul shall thine keep company to heaven.
    Tarry, sweet soul, for mine, then fly abreast,
    As in this glorious and well-foughten field
20   We kept together in our chivalry'.
    Upon these words I came and cheered him up.

Bourbon   To the devil with plans now. I'm going to join the fighting. The shorter the life, the less the shame.

[*They go*]

Scene 6

The noise of battle continues. **King Henry** *and members of his army enter, with some of their prisoners.*

King Henry   We have done well, thrice-valiant countrymen. But the work's not finished; the French are fighting on.

Exeter   The Duke of York sends his respects to Your Majesty.

King Henry   He's still alive? Three times in the past hour I've seen him fall. Three times he was up again and fighting. From his helmet to his spurs, he was a mass of blood.

Exeter   In which robes, brave soldier, he now lies, garnishing the earth. And by his bloody side, yoked to him in honour through his wounds, the noble Earl of Suffolk also lies. Suffolk died first. York, hacked to pieces, came to him where he lay soaked in blood, and took him by the beard, kissing the gaping gashes that bled upon his face. He cried out 'Wait, cousin Suffolk. My soul will go with yours to heaven. Wait, sweet soul, for mine: then fly at my side just as we stood together in chivalry on this glorious and well-fought field'. On hearing these

He smiled me in the face, raught me his hand,
And with a feeble grip says, 'Dear my lord,
Commend my service to my sovereign'.
25   So did he turn, and over Suffolk's neck
He threw his wounded arm, and kissed his lips,
And so espoused to death, with blood he sealed
A testament of noble-ending love.
The pretty and sweet manner of it forced
30   Those waters from me which I would have stopped.
But I had not so much of man in me,
And all my mother came into mine eyes
And gave me up to tears.

King Henry   I blame you not
35   For hearing this I must perforce compound
With mistful eyes, or they will issue too.

[*Alarum*]

But hark, what new alarum is this same?
The French have reinforced their scattered men.
Then every soldier kill his prisoners.
40   Give the word through.

Pistol   *Coup' la gorge.*

[Exeunt]

Scene 7

Another part of the field. Enter **Fluellen** *and* **Gower**.

Fluellen   Kill the poys and the luggage! 'Tis expressly
against the law of arms. 'Tis as arrant a piece of
knavery, mark you now, as can be offert. In your
conscience now, is it not?

words, I came and comforted him. He smiled in my
face, gave me his hand, and with a feeble grip said
'My dear lord, commend my service to my King'.
Then he turned, and threw his wounded arm over
Suffolk's neck, and kissed his lips; and so wedded
to death, he sealed with blood a testament of nobly-
ending love. The gallant and becoming manner of it
overcame my manly resistance; the woman in me
came into my eyes, and I surrendered to my tears.

King Henry   I cannot blame you. Hearing this, I must
choke back my tears, or I will shed them too.

[*The noise of battle suddenly increases*]

Listen, is this a new attack? The French have rallied
their scattered men. Tell every soldier to kill his
prisoners. Pass the word.

Pistol   Cut their throats!

[*They go*]

Scene 7

Fluellen *and* **Gower** *enter in great distress.*

Fluellen   To kill the boys and the camp-followers! It's
expressly against the rules of war. It's the dirtiest bit
of work, look you, that can be done. Upon your
conscience now, is it not?

5 **Gower** 'Tis certain there's not a boy left alive. And the
cowardly rascals that ran from the battle ha' done this
slaughter. Besides, they have burned and carried away
all that was in the King's tent; wherefore the King most
worthily hath caused every soldier to cut

10 his prisoner's throat. Oh 'tis a gallant king.

Fluellen Ay, he was porn at Monmouth. Captain Gower,
what call you the town's name where Alexander the Pig
was born?

Gower Alexander the Great.

15 **Fluellen** Why I pray you, is not 'pig' great? The pig or
the great or the mighty or the huge or the magnanimous
are all one reckonings, save the phrase is a little
variations.

Gower I think Alexander the Great was born in Macedon.

20 His father was called Philip of Macedon, as I take it.

Fluellen I think it is Macedon indeed where Alexander is
born. I tell you, captain, if you look in the maps of the
world I warrant you shall find, in the comparisons
between Macedon and Monmouth, that the situations,

25 look you, is both alike. There is a river in Macedon, and
there is also moreover a river at Monmouth. It is called
Wye at Monmouth, but it is out of my prains what is the
name of the other river – but 'tis all one, 'tis alike as my
fingers is to my fingers, and there is salmons in both. If

30 you mark Alexander's life well, Harry of Monmouth's
life is come after it indifferent well. For there is figures
in all things. Alexander, God knows, and you know, in
his rages and his furies and his wraths and his cholers
and his moods and his displeasures and his indignations,

Gower   There's not a boy left alive, that's for sure. The cowardly rascals who ran away from the battle have done this slaughter. They have burned and looted everything that was in the King's tent, too. So the King has rightly ordered every soldier to cut his prisoner's throat. Oh, he's an excellent King!

Fluellen   Yes. He was born at Monmouth . . . Captain Gower, what do you call the town's name where Alexander the Big was born?

Gower   Alexander the Great?

Fluellen   Why, pray: isn't 'big' the same as 'great'? 'The big' or 'the great' or 'the mighty' or 'the huge' or 'the magnanimous' — they are all descriptive labels, variations on a theme.

Gower   I think Alexander the Great was born in Macedon. His father was called Philip of Macedon, so I believe.

Fluellen   I think it was indeed Macedon where Alexander was born. I assure you, Captain, that if you look at a map of the world, I'm sure you will find — in comparing Macedon and Monmouth — that their locations are alike. There is a river at Macedon, and there is also, moreover, a river at Monmouth. It is called Wye at Monmouth, but I can't remember what the name of the other river is. But it doesn't matter: it's as similar as one of my hands is to the other, and there is salmon in both. If you consider Alexander's life carefully, Harry Monmouth's resembles it remarkably. There are likenesses in everything. Alexander, God knows (and you know) in his rage and his fury and his wrath and his anger and his moodiness and his displeasure and his

35   and also being a little intoxicates in his prains, did in his
      ales and his angers, look you, kill his best friend Cleitus –

Gower   Our King is not like him in that. He never killed
      any of his friends.

Fluellen   It is not well done, mark you now, to take the
40   tales out of my mouth ere it is made an end and
      finished. I speak but in the figures and comparisons of
      it. As Alexander killed his friend Cleitus, being in his
      ales and his cups, so also Harry Monmouth, being in his
      right wits and his good judgements, turned away the fat
45   knight with the great-belly doublet. He was full of jests
      and gipes and knaveries and mocks – I have forgot his
      name –

Gower   Sir John Falstaff.

Fluellen   That is he. I'll tell you, there is good men porn
50   at Monmouth.

Gower   Here comes his majesty.

[*Alarum. Enter the* **King, Warwick, Gloucester, Exeter,**
and soldiers with prisoners. Flourish]

King Henry   I was not angry since I came to France
      Until this instant. Take a trumpet, herald;
      Ride thou unto the horsemen on yond hill.
55   If they will fight with us, bid them come down,
      Or void the field: they do offend our sight.
      If they'll do neither, we will come to them,
      And make them skirr away as swift as stones
      Enforced from the old Assyrian slings.
60   Besides, we'll cut the throats of those we have,
      And not a man of them that we shall take
      Shall taste our mercy. Go and tell them so.

indignation (and also being a little sozzled with drink), did kill (while drunk and angry, look you) his best friend, Cleitus –

Gower   Our King is not like him in that respect! He never killed any of his friends!

Fluellen   It's not polite, look you, to cut my story short before I've finished it completely. I'm only speaking figuratively and metaphorically. Just as Alexander killed his friend Cleitus (being drunk and in his cups) so also Harry Monmouth (being totally sober) turned away the fat knight with the enormous pot belly: he was full of jokes and jibes and mischief and mockery – I've forgotten his name . . .

Gower   Sir John Falstaff.

Fluellen   That's him. I tell you, there are good men born at Monmouth.

Gower   Here comes his majesty.

[**King Henry** *enters, with* **Warwick, Gloucester, Exeter,** *and* **Soldiers** *guarding* **prisoners**]

King Henry   I have not been angry since I came to France, till now. Take a trumpet, Herald. Ride over to the cavalry on the hill over there. If they will fight with us, tell them to come down, or else leave the battlefield: they offend our sight. If they'll do neither, we'll go to them and make them shift as fast as stones flung from the old Assyrian slings. What's more, we'll cut the throats of the prisoners we have, and show no mercy to a single man we take. Go and tell them so.

[*Enter* **Montjoy**]

Exeter   Here comes the herald of the French, my liege.

Gloucester   His eyes are humbler than they used to be.

65 **King Henry**   How now, what means this, herald?
          Know'st thou not
          That I have fined these bones of mine for ransom?
          Com'st thou again for ransom?

Montjoy   No, great King
70   I come to thee for charitable licence,
          That we may wander o'er this bloody field
          To book our dead and then to bury them;
          To sort our nobles from our common men –
          For many of our princes – woe the while! –
75   Lie drowned and soaked in mercenary blood.
          So do our vulgar drench their peasant limbs
          In blood of princes, and our wounded steeds
          Fret fetlock-deep in gore, and with wild rage
          Yerk out their armed heels at their dead masters,
80   Killing them twice. Oh give us leave, great King,
          To view the field in safety, and dispose
          Of their dead bodies.

King Henry   I tell thee truly, herald.
          I know not if the day be ours or no,
85   For yet a many of your horsemen peer
          And gallop o'er the field.

Montjoy   The day is yours.

King Henry   Praised be God, and not our strength, for it.
          What is this castle called that stands hard by?

90 **Montjoy**   They call it Agincourt.

[**Montjoy** *enters*]

Exeter   Here comes the French herald, my liege.

Gloucester   His eyes are humbler than they used to be.

King Henry   Well now, what does this mean, herald? Don't you know I've pledged these bones of mine as my only ransom? Have you come again for ransom money?

Montjoy   No, great King. I come to you for permission, out of your charity, to wander round this field of blood, to record our dead and then to bury them; to sort out nobles from our commoners; for many of our princes, sad to say, lie drowned and soaked in the blood of mercenaries. Thus, our common soldiers soak their base-born limbs in the blood of princes, and our wounded horses writhe fetlock-deep in gore, kicking out at their dead masters with their steel-shod hooves, killing them a second time. Oh, give us your consent, great King, to survey the battlefield in safety, and to dispose of the dead bodies.

King Henry   Frankly, herald, I do not know whether we have won the day or not. Many of your horsemen can still be seen galloping across the field.

Montjoy   Victory is yours.

King Henry   Praise be to God, and not our army, for it. What is the castle called nearby?

Montjoy   They call it Agincourt.

King Henry   Then call we this the field of Agincourt,
Fought on the day of Crispin Crispianus.

Fluellen   Your grandfather of famous memory, an't please
your majesty, and your great-uncle Edward the Plack
95   Prince of Wales, as I have read in the chronicles, fought
a most prave pattle here in France.

King Henry   They did, Fluellen.

Fluellen   Your majesty says very true. If your majesties is
remembered of it, the Welshmen did good service in a
100   garden where leeks did grow, wearing leeks in their
Monmouth caps, which your majesty know to this hour
is an honourable badge of the service. And I do believe
your majesty takes no scorn to wear the leek upon Saint
Tavy's day.

105 **King Henry**   I wear it for a memorable honour,
For I am Welsh, you know, good countryman.

Fluellen   All the water in Wye cannot wash your majesty's
Welsh plood out of your pody, I can tell you that. God
pless it and preserve it, as long as it pleases his grace,
110   and his majesty too.

King Henry   Thanks, good my countryman.

Fluellen   By Jeshu, I am your majesty's countryman. I
care not who know it, I will confess it to all the world. I
need not be ashamed of your majesty, praised be God,
115   so long as your majesty is an honest man.

King Henry   God keep me so. Our heralds go with him.
Bring me just notice of the numbers dead
On both our parts. [*Pointing to* **Williams**] Call yonder
fellow hither.

King Henry Then we'll call this 'The Battle of
Agincourt', fought on St Crispin's day.

Fluellen Your grandfather of famous memory, may it
please your majesty, and your great uncle Edward
the Black Prince of Wales, according to what I've
read in the history books, fought a most brave
battle here.

King Henry They did, Fluellen.

Fluellen Your Majesty is right. If Your Majesty recalls,
the Welsh fought well in a garden where leeks were
growing, wearing leeks in their Monmouth [*ie flat,
round*] caps, which Your Majesty knows is an
honourable badge of service to this day. I do
believe Your Majesty is proud to wear the leek on
St David's day.

King Henry I wear it as a mark of respect, because I
am Welsh, you know, good countryman.

Fluellen All the water in the River Wye cannot wash
the Welsh blood out of Your Majesty's body, I can
tell you that. God bless and preserve it, as long as it
is His will, and Your Majesty's too.

King Henry Thanks, my good countryman!

Fluellen By Jesus, I am Your Majesty's countryman,
and I don't care who knows it. I will admit it to all
the world. I needn't be ashamed of Your Majesty,
praise be to God, so long as Your Majesty stays an
honest man.

King Henry God keep me so. Send our heralds with
him; bring me an accurate report of the death-roll
on both sides.

120 **Exeter**   Soldier, you must come to the King.

King Henry   Soldier, why wearest thou that glove in thy
cap?

Williams   An't please your majesty, 'tis the gage of one
that I should fight withal, if he be alive.

125 **King Henry**   An Englishman?

Williams   An't please your majesty, a rascal, that
swaggered with me last night – who, if a live, and ever
dare to challenge this glove, I had sworn to take him a
box o'th'ear; or if I can see my glove in his cap – which
130 he swore, as he was a soldier, he would wear if a lived –
I will strike it out soundly.

King Henry   What think you, Captain Fluellen? Is it fit
this soldier keep his oath?

Fluellen   He is a craven and a villain else, an't please
135 your majesty, in my conscience.

King Henry   It may be his enemy is a gentleman of great
sort, quite from the answer of his degree.

Fluellen   Though he be as good a gentleman as the devil
is, as Lucifer and Beelzebub himself, it is necessary, look
140 your grace, that he keep his vow and his oath. If he be
perjured, see you now, his reputation is as arrant a
villain and a jack-sauce as ever his black shoe trod upon
God's ground and his earth, in my conscience, law.

[**Montjoy** *leaves, with a* **Herald**. **Henry** *notices that*
Williams *is present amongst his soldiers, and*
wearing a glove in his cap]

Call that fellow over here!

Exeter Soldier, you must come to the King.

King Henry Soldier, why are you wearing that glove
in your cap?

Williams With respect, Your Majesty, it's a gauntlet
belonging to a man I should fight with, if he's alive.

King Henry An Englishman?

Williams With respect, Your Majesty, a rascal, who
put on airs with me last night. If he has survived,
and ever dares to challenge this glove, I've sworn to
box his ears; or if I can see my glove in his cap —
which he swore on his soldier's honour he would
wear if he came through — I'll knock it out, and no
messing.

King Henry What do you think, Captain Fluellen?
Should this soldier keep his oath?

Fluellen He's a coward and a villain, with respect to
Your Majesty, if he doesn't, upon my conscience!

King Henry It could be that his enemy is a gentleman
of high rank, unable to respond to a man of lower
degree.

Fluellen Even if he's as fine a gentleman as the devil
is — as Lucifer or Beelzebub himself — it is
necessary, look Your Grace, that he keeps to his
vow and his oath. If he perjures himself, d'you see,
he'd have the reputation for being as arrant a villain
and as saucy a knave as ever trod upon God's

King Henry   Then keep thy vow, sirrah, when thou
145   meetest the fellow.

Williams   So I will, my liege, as I live.

King Henry   Who serv'st thou under?

Williams   Under Captain Gower, my liege.

Fluellen   Gower is a good captain, and is good knowledge
150   and literatured in the wars.

King Henry   Call him hither to me, soldier.

Williams   I will, my liege.

[Exit

King Henry   Here, Fluellen, wear thou this favour for me
and stick it in thy cap. When Alençon and myself were
155   down together, I plucked this glove from his helm. If any
man challenge this, he is a friend to Alençon and an
enemy to our person. If thou encounter any such,
apprehend him, an thou dost me love.

Fluellen   Your grace does me as great honours as can be
160   desired in the hearts of his subjects. I would fain see the
man that has but two legs that shall find himself
aggriefed at this glove, that is all; but I would fain see it
once. And please God of his grace, that I might see it.

King Henry   Know'st thou Gower?

165 **Fluellen**   He is my dear friend, an't please you.

ground and God's earth in black shoes, upon my
conscience, lord save me!

King Henry   Then keep to your vow, man, when you
meet the fellow.

Williams   So I will, my liege, upon my life.

King Henry   Who is your commanding officer?

Williams   Captain Gower, my liege.

Fluellen   Gower is a good captain, well experienced
and well read in warfare.

King Henry   Call him here to me, soldier.

Williams   I will, my liege.

[*He goes*]

King Henry   Here, Fluellen, wear this keepsake for me
[*he hands* **Fluellen** *the glove which* **Williams** *gave
him earlier*] and stick it in your cap. When the Duke
of Alençon and I were fighting on foot together, I
snatched this glove from his helmet. If any man
takes up this challenge, he is a friend of Alençon
and an enemy of mine. If you encounter any such,
arrest him, if you love me.

Fluellen   Your grace does me as great an honour as
one of his subjects could have as his heart's desire.
I'd like to see the man with two legs that takes
offence at this glove, that's all, just once. May it
please God of His grace to grant me that!

King Henry   Do you know Gower?

Fluellen   He is my dear friend, with respect.

King Henry   Pray thee, go seek him and bring him to my
tent.

Fluellen   I will fetch him.

[*Exit*

King Henry   My lord of Warwick and my brother
170   Gloucester,
Follow Fluellen closely at the heels.
The glove which I have given him for a favour
May haply purchase him a box o'th'ear.
It is the soldier's. I by bargain should
175   Wear it myself. Follow, good cousin Warwick.
If that the soldier strike him, as I judge
By his blunt bearing he will keep his word,
Some sudden mischief may arise of it.
For I do know Fluellen valiant
180   And touched with choler, hot as gunpowder,
And quickly will return an injury.
Follow, and see there be no harm between them.
Go you with me, uncle of Exeter.

[*Exeunt*

Scene 8

King Henry's pavilion. Enter **Gower** *and* **Williams**.

Williams   I warrant it is to knight you, captain.

[*Enter* **Fluellen**]

Fluellen   God's will and his pleasure, captain, I beseech
you now, come apace to the King. There is more good
toward you, peradventure, than is in your knowledge to
5   dream of.

King Henry   Pray go seek him, and bring him to my tent.

Fluellen   I will fetch him.

[*He goes*]

King Henry   My lord of Warwick and my brother Gloucester, follow closely on Fluellen's heels. The glove which I have given him to wear as a favour may perhaps gain him a box over the ears. It is the soldier's. I ought to wear it myself to keep my bargain. Follow him, good cousin Warwick. If the soldier should strike him, and I deduce from his blunt manner that he'll keep his word, there might be a sudden brawl. I know Fluellen is courageous and short-tempered, touchy as gunpowder, and he'll quickly return an insult. Follow, and see that no harm comes between them. Uncle of Exeter, go with me.

[*They depart*]

Scene 8

Outside the King's tent. **Williams** *enters with* **Captain Gower.**

Williams   I'll bet it is to knight you, Captain!

[**Fluellen** *meets them*]

Fluellen   God's will and pleasure, Captain, I beg you now, come quickly to the King. There's prospects awaiting you, surely, that are beyond your wildest dreams.

Williams   Sir, know you this glove?

Fluellen   Know the glove? I know the glove is a glove.

Williams   I know this, and thus I challenge it.

[*He strikes* **Fluellen**]

Fluellen   'Sblud, an arrant traitor as any's in the universal
10   world, or in France, or in England.

Gower   How now, sir? You villain!

Williams   Do you think I'll be forsworn?

Fluellen   Stand away, Captain Gower. I will give treason
his payment into plows, I warrant you.

15   **Williams**   I am no traitor.

Fluellen   That's a lie in thy throat. I charge you in his
majesty's name, apprehend him. He's a friend of the
Duke Alençon's.

[*Enter* **Warwick** *and* **Gloucester**]

Warwick   How now, how now, what's the matter?

20   **Fluellen**   My lord of Warwick, here is – praised be God for
it – a most contagious treason come to light, look you, as
you shall desire in a summer's day. Here is his majesty.

[*Enter the* **King** *and* **Exeter**]

King Henry   How now, what's the matter?

222

Williams   [*observing the matching glove in* **Fluellen's** *cap, and removing the one he is wearing*] Sir, do you know this glove?

Fluellen   Know the glove? I know the glove is a glove.

Williams   I know this one! [*He grabs the glove from* **Fluellen's** *cap*] Here's my challenge! [*He hits* **Fluellen**]

Fluellen   By God! You're as downright a traitor as any in the whole wide world, or in France, or in England!

Gower   [*to* **Williams**] What, man? You villain!

Williams   Do you think I'll be defamed?

Fluellen   Stand aside, Captain Gower. I'll give treason his payment in blows, I promise you!

Williams   I'm no traitor!

Fluellen   That's a damned lie. In His Majesty's name, arrest him! He's a friend of the Duke of Alençon!

[*The* **Earl of Warwick** *and the* **Duke of Gloucester** *enter*]

Warwick   Now, now; what's the matter?

Fluellen   My lord of Warwick: here is – praise be to God for it! – the most pestilential treason brought to light, look you, as you'd ever desire to see on a summer's day. Here is His Majesty.

[**King Henry** *and the* **Duke of Exeter** *enter*]

King Henry   [*in mock surprise*] What's going on here?

Fluellen   My liege, here is a villain and a traitor that, look
25   your grace, has struck the glove which your majesty is
take out of the helmet of Alençon.

Williams   My liege, this was my glove – here is the fellow
of it – and he that I gave it to in change promised to
wear it in his cap. I promised to strike him, if he did. I
30   met this man with my glove in his cap, and I have been
as good as my word.

Fluellen   Your majesty hear now, saving your majesty's
manhood, what an arrant, rascally, beggarly, lousy
knave it is. I hope your majesty is pear me testimony
35   and witness, and will avouchment that this is the glove
of Alençon that your majesty is give me, in your
conscience now.

King Henry   Give me thy glove, soldier. Look, here is
the fellow of it.
40   'Twas I indeed thou promised'st to strike,
And thou hast given me most bitter terms.

Fluellen   An't please your majesty, let his neck answer for
it, if there is any martial law in the world.

King Henry   How canst thou make me satisfaction?

45   **Williams**   All offences, my lord, come from the heart.
Never came any from mine that might offend your
majesty.

King Henry   It was ourself thou didst abuse.

Williams   Your majesty came not like yourself. You
50   appeared to me but as a common man. Witness the
night, your garments, your lowliness. And what your
highness suffered under that shape, I beseech you take it
for your own fault, and not mine, for had you been as I

Fluellen   My liege, here is the villain and the traitor
who has struck the glove Your Majesty took from
Alençon's helmet.

Williams   My liege, this was my glove [*showing the
one taken from* **Fluellen**] and here is the matching
one. [*He indicates the other*] The man I gave it to in
exchange promised to wear it in his cap. I promised
to strike him if he did. I met this man with my glove
in his cap, and I have been as good as my word.

Fluellen   Your Majesty: just listen, with respect to
Your Majesty's manhood, to what an out-and-out
rascally beggarly lousy rogue he is! I hope Your
Majesty will bear me testimony and witness, and
will confirm, that this is the glove of Alencon which
Your Majesty gave me, in all conscience.

King Henry   Give me the glove you have, soldier.
look; here is its match. It was none other than me
you promised to strike, and you have spoken very
critically of me.

Fluellen   Let him hang for it, so please Your Majesty,
if there is any military law in the world.

King Henry   How can you make amends?

Williams   All offences, my lord, come from the heart.
None ever came from mine that might give offence
to Your Majesty.

King Henry   You abused me personally.

Williams   Your Majesty came in disguise. You
appeared to me just as a commoner: witness the
time of night, your clothes and your lowly manner.
Whatever your highness suffered as a result, I beg
you to accept as your own fault and not mine;

took you for, I had made no offence. Therefore I beseech
55   your highness pardon me.

King Henry   Here, Uncle Exeter, fill this glove with
   crowns
And give it to this fellow. Keep it, fellow,
And wear it for an honour in thy cap
60   Till I do challenge it. Give him the crowns.
And captain, you must needs be friends with him.

Fluellen   By this day and this light, the fellow has mettle
enough in his belly. Hold, there is twelve pence for you,
and I pray you serve God, and keep you out of prawls
65   and prabbles and quarrels and dissensions, and I
warrant you it is the better for you.

Williams   I will none of your money.

Fluellen   It is with a good will. I can tell you, it will serve
you to mend your shoes. Come, wherefore should you be
70   so pashful? Your shoes is not so good. 'Tis a good silling,
I warrant you, or I will change it.

[*Enter an English* **Herald**]

King Henry   Now, herald, are the dead numbered?

Herald   Here is the number of the slaughtered French.

King Henry   What prisoners of good sort are taken, uncle?

75 **Exeter**   Charles, Duke of Orleans, nephew to the King;
John, Duke of Bourbon, and Lord Boucicault;
Of other lords and barons, knights and squires,
Full fifteen hundred, besides common men.

because had you been what I thought you were, I would have committed no offence. Therefore I beseech Your Highness to pardon me.

King Henry   Here, Uncle Exeter: fill this glove with gold coins and give it to this fellow. Keep it, man, and wear it in your cap as an honour till such time as I challenge it. [*To* **Exeter**, *who hesitates in surprise*] Give him the crowns! [*To* **Fluellen**] And Captain, you must make friends with him.

Fluellen   By this day and this sunlight, this fellow has guts! [*Searching his purse*] Hold on, there's some money for you; and I hope you'll serve God, and keep out of brawls and squabbles and quarrels and altercations, and it'll be the better for you.

Williams   I don't want your money.

Fluellen   [*pushing it on him*] It is given willingly. You can have your shoes mended, I can tell you. [**Williams** *still hesitates*] Come – why should you be so bashful? Your shoes aren't up to much. It's a genuine coin, I guarantee you, or I'll change it. [**Williams** *relents*]

[*A* **Herald** *enters*]

King Henry   Now, Herald: have the dead been counted?

Herald   Here is the count of the slaughtered French.

[*He hands the* **King** *a scroll*]

King Henry   What high-ranking prisoners have we taken, Uncle?

Exeter   Charles, Duke of Orleans, the King's nephew. John, Duke of Bourbon, and Lord Boucicault. Fully fifteen hundred other lords, barons, knights and squires, besides men of low degree.

King Henry   This note doth tell me of ten thousand
80   French
        That in the field lie slain. Of princes in this number
        And nobles bearing banners, there lie dead
        One hundred twenty-six; added to these,
        Of knights, esquires, and gallant gentlemen,
85   Eight thousand and four hundred, of the which
        Five hundred were but yesterday dubbed knights.
        So that in these ten thousand they have lost
        There are but sixteen hundred mercenaries;
        The rest are princes, barons, lords, knights, squires,
90   And gentlemen of blood and quality.
        The names of those their nobles that lie dead:
        Charles Delabret, High Constable of France;
        Jacques of Chatillon, Admiral of France;
        The Master of the Crossbows, Lord Rambures;
95   Great Master of France, the brave Sir Guiscard
            Dolfin:
        John, Duke of Alençon; Antony, Duke of Brabant,
        The brother to the Duke of Burgundy;
        And Edward, Duke of Bar; of lusty earls,
100   Grandpré and Roussi, Fauconbridge and Foix,
        Beaumont and Marle, Vaudemont and Lestrelles.
        Here was a royal fellowship of death.
        Where is the number of our English dead?

        [*He is given another paper*]

        Edward the Duke of York, the Earl of Suffolk,
105   Sir Richard Ketley, Davy Gam Esquire;
        None else of name, and of all other men
        But five-and-twenty. Oh God, thy arm was here,
        And not to us, but to thy arm alone
        Ascribe we all. When, without stratagem,
110   But in plain shock and even play of battle,

King Henry   This tells me that ten thousand
Frenchmen were slain in the battle. Amongst them
were one hundred and twenty-six princes and
nobles carrying banners; as well as eight thousand
four hundred knights, squires, and gallant
gentlemen, five hundred of whom were knighted
only yesterday. So of the ten thousand they have
lost, there are only sixteen hundred mercenaries:
the rest are princes, barons, lords, knights, squires,
and gentlemen of rank and quality. The names of
those of their nobles who lie dead: Charles
Delabret, High Constable of France; Jacques of
Chatillon, Admiral of France; the Master of the
Crossbows, Lord Rambures; the brave Sir Guiscard
Dolfin, Master of the Royal Household; John, Duke
of Alençon; Antony, Duke of Brabant, the Duke of
Burgundy's brother; and Edward, Duke of Bar. Of
spirited Earls: Grandpré and Roussi, Fauconbridge
and Foix, Beaumont and Marle, Vaudemont and
Lestrelles. Here was a royal comradeship in death!
Where is the number of English dead?

[*The* **Herald** *hands him a second scroll*]

Edward, Duke of York; the Earl of Suffolk; Sir
Richard Ketley; Davy Gam, Esquire. Nobody else of
noble birth, and only twenty-five other men. Oh
God, your might was present here, and to it alone
and not to us we attribute everything. When — not
counting ambushes, but in the plain give-and-take

Was ever known so great and little loss
On one part and on th'other? Take it God,
For it is none but thine.

Exeter   'Tis wonderful

115 **King Henry**   Come, go we in procession to the village,
And be it death proclaimed through our host
To boast of this, or take that praise from God
Which is his only.

Fluellen   Is it not lawful, an't please your majesty, to tell
120   how many is killed?

King Henry   Yes, captain, but with this acknowledgement,
That God fought for us.

Fluellen   Yes, in my conscience, he did us great good.

King Henry   Do we all holy rites:
125   Let there be sung Non nobis and Te Deum,
The dead with charity enclosed in clay;
And then to Calais, and to England then,
Where ne'er from France arrived more happy men.

                                              [*Exeunt*]

of battle – was so great and so little loss known on either side? Take credit, God, for it is yours entirely.

Exeter   It is wonderful!

King Henry   Come, we shall go to the village in procession. Proclaim it to our army that it is death to boast of this, or to take from God the praise that is entirely his.

Fluellen   Is it not lawful, so please your Majesty, to say how many were killed?

King Henry   Yes, Captain, but only with this acknowledgement; that God fought for us.

Fluellen   Yes. Upon my conscience, he helped us a lot.

King Henry   We shall celebrate all holy rites: the Non Nobis and Te Deum shall be sung; the dead shall be buried with Christian charity. Then we shall go to Calais and on to England, the happiest men from France ever to arrive there.

[*They leave*]

Act five

Chorus   Vouchsafe to those that have not read the story
        That I may prompt them – and of such as have,
        I humbly pray them to admit th'excuse
        Of time, of numbers, and due course of things,
5   Which cannot in their huge and proper life
        Be here presented. Now we bear the King
        Toward Calais. Grant him there; there seen,
        Heave him away upon your winged thoughts
        Athwart the sea. Behold, the English beach
10   Pales in the flood, with men, with wives, and boys,
        Whose shouts and claps out-voice the deep-mouthed sea,
        Which, like a mighty whiffler, fore the King
        Seems to prepare his way. So let him land,
        And solemnly see him set on to London.
15   So swift a pace hath thought, that even now
        You may imagine him upon Blackheath,
        Where that his lords desire him to have borne
        His bruised helmet and his bended sword
        Before him through the city; he forbids it,
20   Being free from vainness and self-glorious pride,
        Giving full trophy, signal, and ostent
        Quite from himself, to God. But now behold,
        In the quick forge and working-house of thought,
        How London doth pour out her citizens.
25   The Mayor and all his brethren, in best sort,
        Like to the senators of th'antique Rome
        With the plebeians swarming at their heels,
        Go forth and fetch their conqu'ring Caesar in –
        As, by a lower but loving likelihood,

Act five

The **Announcer** *enters.*

Announcer   May those who have not read the story
permit me to enlighten them. As for those who
have, I humbly beg them to make due allowance for
the time factor, the many people involved, and the
fine details of events, which cannot in their vastness
and reality be presented in this theatre. Now we
take the King towards Calais. Grant him arrived
there. Having been seen, heave him away across
the sea on the wings of your thoughts. Look! The
English beach fences off the waves with lines of
men, women and boys. Their shouts and clapping
drown the noise of the roaring sea, which seems to
be preparing the King's way like a mighty advance
escort. So, let him land, and see him make for
London in full ceremony. So quick is thought, you
can imagine him now at Blackheath Common,
where his nobles want him to have his dented
helmet and his bent sword carried before him
through the city. He forbids it, being free from
vanity and conceit, giving all credit, honour and
glory to God, and not himself! Now see, using the
living forge and factory of the mind, how London
decants her citizens. The Mayor and his fellow-
councillors, in their best clothes, just like the
Senators of ancient Rome, with the common people
swarming at their heels, go forth and bring in their
conquering Caesar. So would they for a lesser but

30 Were now the General of our gracious Empress –
As in good time he may – from Ireland coming,
Bringing rebellion broached on his sword,
How many would the peaceful city quit
To welcome him! Much more, and much more cause,
35 Did they this Harry. Now in London place him;
As yet the lamentation of the French
Invites the King of England's stay at home.
The Emperor's coming in behalf of France,
To order peace between them. *(. . . . .)
40   and omit
All the occurrences, whatever chanced,
Till Harry's back-return again to France.
There must we bring him, and myself have played
The interim by rememb'ring you 'tis past.
45 Then brook abridgement, and your eyes advance,
After your thoughts, straight back again to France.

[*Exit*

*Some words and/or lines are missing here.

.

Scene 1

France. The English camp. Enter **Gower** *and* **Fluellen.**

Gower   Nay, that's right. But why wear you your leek
today? Saint Davy's day is past.

very desirable probability: if our gracious Queen
Elizabeth's General, the Earl of Essex, should return
from Ireland, as one day he will, the rebellion
crushed by his sword, how many would quit the
peaceful city to welcome him! They welcomed this
Harry even more, and with greater reason.

Now settle him in London, since the sorrowing of
the French disposes the King to stay at home. The
visit of the Holy Roman Emperor on behalf of
France, to order peace between the two countries,
[and the death of the Dauphin, we must ignore]*;
and omit all the intervening campaigns, etc, till we
reach Harry's arrival back again in France.

There we must bring him, and I myself have filled in
the interim by reminding you of what has occurred.
Leap the gap, and look ahead, following your
thoughts, straight back again to France . . .

[He goes]

*Conjecture

Scene 1

The English camp. **Captain Gower** enters, with **Captain
Fluellen**, who is wearing a leek in his cap and carrying
a club.

Gower   I quite agree. But why are you wearing a leek
today? St David's Day has passed.

Fluellen   There is occasions and causes why and wherefore
in all things. I will tell you, ass my friend, Captain
5   Gower. The rascally scald, beggarly, lousy, pragging
knave Pistol – which you and yourself and all the world
knows to be no petter than a fellow, look you now, of no
merits – he is come to me, and prings me pread and salt
yesterday, look you, and bid me eat my leek. It was in a
10   place where I could not breed no contention with him,
but I will be so bold as to wear it in my cap till I see
him once again, and then I will tell him a little piece of
my desires.

[*Enter* **Pistol**]

Gower   Why, here he comes, swelling like a turkey-cock.

15 **Fluellen**   'Tis no matter for his swellings nor his turkey-
cocks. God pless you Ancient Pistol, you scurvy, lousy
knave, God pless you.

Pistol   Ha, art thou bedlam? Dost thou thirst, base
Trojan,
20   To have me fold up Parca's fatal web?
Hence! I am qualmish at the smell of leek.

Fluellen   I peseech you heartily, scurvy, lousy knave, at
my desires and my requests and my petitions, to eat,
look you, this leek. Because, look you, you do not love
25   it, nor your affections and your appetites and your
digestions does not agree with it, I would desire you to
eat it.

Pistol   Not for Cadwallader and all his goats.

Fluellen   There is one goat for you. [*He strikes* **Pistol**] Will
30   you be so good, scald knave, as eat it?

Fluellen   There are reasons and causes, whys and wherefores, in everything. I shall tell you, as my friend, Captain Gower. The rascally, scurvy, beggarly, lousy, bragging rogue Pistol – who you yourself and all the world knows to be no better than a fellow, look you, of no merits – he came to me, and brought me bread and salt yesterday, look you, and told me to eat my leek. It was at a place where I couldn't answer him back, but I'll be so bold as to wear it in my cap till I see him once again, and then I'll give him a little piece of my mind.

[**Pistol** *enters*]

Gower   Why, here he comes, strutting like a turkey-cock.

Fluellen   I don't care about his struttings or his turkey-cocks. [*Turning to* **Pistol**, *polite as a shark*] God bless you Ensign Pistol, you scurvy lousy rogue, God bless you.

Pistol   What, are you mad? Is it your desire, you drunken tosspot, to have me terminate your life? Begone! I am nauseated by the smell of leek.

Fluellen   I heartily beg you, scurvy lousy rogue – at my desire and my request and my entreaty – to eat, look you, this leek. Because, look you, you don't like it; nor does it agree with your taste, your appetite and your digestion, I wish you to eat it.

Pistol   Not for King Cadwallader and his flock of goats! [*A taunt, implying that the Welsh are a primitive people*]

Fluellen   [*hitting* **Pistol** *hard with his club*] There's one goat for you! Will you be so good, scurvy rogue, as to eat it?

237

Pistol   Base Trojan, thou shalt die.

Fluellen   You say very true, scald knave, when God's will
is. I will desire you to live in the mean time, and eat
your victuals. Come, there is sauce for it. [*He strikes him*]
35   You called me yesterday 'mountain-squire', but I will
make you today 'a squire of low degree'. I pray you, fall
to. If you can mock a leek you can eat a leek.

Gower   Enough, captain, you have astonished him.

Fluellen   I say, I will make him eat some part of my leek,
40   or I will peat his pate four days and four nights. Bite, I
pray you. It is good for your green wound and your
ploody coxcomb.

Pistol   Must I bite?

Fluellen   Yes, certainly, and out of doubt and out of
45   question too, and ambiguities.

Pistol   By this leek, I will most horribly revenge – I eat
and eat – I swear –

Fluellen   Eat, I pray you. Will you have some more sauce
to your leek? There is not enough leek to swear by.

50 **Pistol**   Quiet thy cudgel, thou dost see I eat.

Fluellen   Much good do you, scald knave, heartily. Nay,
pray you throw none away. The skin is good for your
broken coxcomb. When you take occasions to see leeks
hereafter, I pray you mock at 'em, that is all.

Pistol Reprobate. You shall die!

Fluellen Very true, scurvy rogue: when it is God's
will. I wish you to live in the meantime, and eat
your food. Come, [*hitting him again*] there's the
sauce for it. Yesterday you called me 'Squire
Wasteland'. Today I'll make you 'Squire Kneebend'.
[*He beats him till he falls to his knees*] Pray tuck in!
If you can mock a leek, you can eat a leek. [*He
strikes* **Pistol** *repeatedly, drawing blood*]

Gower That's enough, Captain. You have stunned
him.

Fluellen I say I'll make him eat some part of my leek,
or I'll thump his head for four days and four nights.
Bite, if you please! It is good for your raw wound
and your cut head.

Pistol Must I bite?

Fluellen Yes, certainly, and beyond all doubt, and out
of all question too, and all uncertainty.

Pistol By this leek, I shall most horribly revenge –
[**Fluellen** *lifts his club*] I'm eating – I'm eating! I
swear it!

Fluellen Eat, I beg you. Will you have some more
sauce for your leek? You haven't got enough leek to
swear by.

Pistol Keep that club still. You can see I'm eating.

Fluellen Much good may it do you, scurvy rogue,
heartily! Now, please don't throw any away. The
skin is good for your fractured skull. Whenever you
see leeks from now on, just mock them, I beg you:
that's all!

55 **Pistol**   Good.

Fluellen   Ay, leeks is good. Hold you, there is a groat to
heal your pate.

Pistol   Me, a groat?

Fluellen   Yes, verily, and in truth you shall take it, or I
60   have another leek in my pocket which you shall eat.

Pistol   I take thy groat in earnest of revenge.

Fluellen   If I owe you anything, I will pay you in cudgels.
You shall be a woodmonger, and buy nothing of me but
cudgels. God b'wi'you, and keep you, and heal your
65   pate.

[*Exit*

Pistol   All hell shall stir for this.

Gower   Go, go, you are a counterfeit cowardly knave. Will
you mock at an ancient tradition, begun upon an
honourable respect and worn as a memorable trophy of
70   predeceased valour, and dare not avouch in your deeds
any of your words? I have seen you gleeking and galling
at this gentleman twice or thrice. You thought, because
he could not speak English in the native garb, he could
not therefore handle an English cudgel. You find it
75   otherwise. And henceforth let a Welsh correction teach
you a good English condition. Fare ye well.

[*Exit*]

Pistol   Doth Fortune play the hussy with me now?
News have I that my Doll is dead i'th'spital
Of malady of France,
80   And there my rendezvous is quite cut off.

240

Pistol   [*Anything to get away*] They're good.

Fluellen   Yes, leeks taste good. Hold on, there's a copper coin for you, to heal your head.

Pistol   Me, a copper coin?

Fluellen   Yes, indeed, and you will indeed take it, or I have another leek in my pocket which you shall eat. [*He produces a giant one, to* **Pistol***'s horror*]

Pistol   I'll take your coin: as part-payment of my revenge!

Fluellen   If I owe you anything, I'll pay you in clubs. [*Wielding his leek again threateningly*] You must become a timber-merchant, and get your clubs from me. [*Benignly*] God go with you, and keep you safe, and heal your head.

[*He goes*]

Pistol   There'll be hell to pay for this!

Gower   Be off with you: you are a deceitful cowardly rascal! Will you mock an ancient tradition, started to commemorate the valiant dead and worn in their honour and not back your words with deeds? I have seen you mocking and scoffing at this gentleman two or three times. Because he could not speak English like a native, you thought he therefore could not handle an English club. You've found it otherwise. Henceforth, let a Welsh hiding teach you to behave like a good Englishman. Farewell.

[*He goes*]

Pistol   Is Lady Luck playing whore's tricks with me now? I've had news that my Doll is dead of the pox, in the poor ward, so I've no home to go to. I'm

241

Old I do wax, and from my weary limbs
Honour is cudgelled. Well, bawd I'll turn,
And something lean to cutpurse of quick hand.
To England will I steal, and there I'll steal,
85   And patches will I get unto these cudgelled scars,
And swear I got them in the Gallia wars.

[*Exi.*

Scene 2

France. The French King's palace. Enter at one door **King Henry, Exeter, Clarence, Warwick,** *and other lords; at another, the* **French King, Queen Isabel,** *the* **Duke of Burgundy, Princess Katherine, Alice** *and others.*

King Henry   Peace to this meeting, wherefore we are met!
Unto our brother France and to our sister,
Health and fair time of day. Joy and good wishes
To our most fair and princely cousin Katherine;
5   And as a branch and member of this royalty,
By whom this great assembly is contrived,
We do salute you, Duke of Burgundy.
And princes French, and peers, health to you all!

French King   Right joyous are we to behold your face.
10   Most worthy brother England, fairly met.
So are you, princes English, every one.

growing old, and Honour has been thrashed out of my weary limbs. Well, I'll become a pimp, and try my hand at pickpocketing. I'll slip off back to England, where I'll steal. And I'll put plasters on the scars where I was thrashed, and swear I got them in the French wars.

[*He goes*]

Scene 2

The palace of King Charles VI in France. At one door, **King Henry** *enters, accompanied by the* **Duke of Exeter**, *the* **Duke of Clarence**, *the* **Earl of Warwick**, *and other lords. Through the opposite door,* **King Charles VI of France** *enters with* **Queen Isabel**, *and other French nobles, among them* **Princess Katherine** *and* **Alice** *her maid. The* **Duke of Burgundy** *follows them. He is the peacemaker.*

King Henry   Peace be to this conference; the reason for our meeting. Health and greetings to the King and Queen of France. Joy and good wishes to our most beautiful Princess Katherine. And as a member of this royal family, and the convenor of this great assembly, we salute you, Duke of Burgundy. French princes and nobles: health to you all!

King Charles   We rejoice to see you. Most worthy England, our meeting is most welcome. So are you, English princes, every one.

Queen Isabel   So happy be the issue, brother England,
Of this good day and of this gracious meeting,
And we are now glad to behold your eyes –
15 Your eyes which hitherto have borne in them,
Against the French that met them in their bent,
The fatal balls of murdering basilisks.
The venom of such looks we fairly hope
Have lost their quality, and that this day
20 Shall change all griefs and quarrels into love.

King Henry   To cry amen to that, thus we appear.

Queen Isabel   You English princes all, I do salute you.

Burgundy   My duty to you both, on equal love,
Great Kings of France and England. That I have
25   laboured
With all my wits, my pains, and strong endeavours,
To bring your most imperial majesties
Unto this bar and royal interview,
Your mightiness on both parts best can witness.
30 Since, then, my office hath so far prevailed
That face to face and royal eye to eye
You have congreeted, let it not disgrace me
If I demand before this royal view,
What rub or what impediment there is
35 Why that the naked, poor, and mangled peace,
Dear nurse of arts, plenties, and joyful births,
Should not in this best garden of the world,
Our fertile France, put up her lovely visage?
Alas, she hath from France too long been chased,
40 And all her husbandry doth lie on heaps,
Corrupting in its own fertility.
Her vine, the merry cheerer of the heart,
Unpruned dies; her hedges even-pleached
Like prisoners wildly overgrown with hair

Queen Isabel   May the outcome of this auspicious day
and gracious meeting, dear England, be as happy as
we are now glad to see your eyes, which hitherto
have possessed the fatal powers of cannons and of
basilisks [*mythical reptiles whose looks were said to
kill*] when focused in anger on the French. We feel
sure that the venom of these looks has lost its sting,
and that this day will change all former griefs and
quarrels into love.

King Henry   We are here to say 'amen' to that.

Queen Isabel   English princes all, I salute you.

Burgundy   [*opening the conference*] Great Kings of
France and England: my service to you both, with
equal love! Your Highnesses on both sides can best
confirm that I have laboured with all my skill,
diligence, and energy to bring your most imperial
majesties to this royal high-level conference. Since,
then, my good offices have prevailed upon you to
meet face-to-face and royal eye-to-eye, do not fault
me if I ask in your royal presence what grievance,
or what impediment, there is preventing Peace – so
naked, poor and mangled, the dear nourisher of
Arts, prosperity and happy parenthood – from
showing her lovely self again in our fertile France,
the world's best garden? Alas, for too long she has
been expelled from France. Her vegetables lie in
heaps, rotting in their own rich compost. Her vines,
the source of merry cheerfulness, die unpruned. Her
trim hedges, like prisoners with wildly unkempt

45   Put forth disordered twigs; her fallow leas
     The darnel, hemlock, and rank fumitory
     Doth root upon, while that the coulter rusts
     That should deracinate such savagery.
     The even mead – that erst brought sweetly forth
50   The freckled cowslip, burnet, and green clover –
     Wanting the scythe, all uncorrected, rank,
     Conceives by idleness, and nothing teems
     But hateful docks, rough thistles, kecksies, burs,
     Losing both beauty and utility.
55   And all our vineyards, fallows, meads, and hedges,
     Defective in their natures, grow to wildness;
     Even so our houses and ourselves and children
     Have lost, or do not learn for want of time,
     The sciences that should become our country,
60   But grow like savages – as soldiers will
     That nothing do but meditate on blood –
     To swearing and stern looks, diffused attire,
     And everything that seems unnatural.
     Which to reduce into our former favour
65   You are assembled, and my speech entreats
     That I may know the let why gentle peace
     Should not expel these inconveniences
     And bless us with her former qualities.

King Henry   If, Duke of Burgundy, you would the peace
70   Whose want gives growth to th'imperfections
     Which you have cited, you must buy that peace
     With full accord to all our just demands,
     Whose tenors and particular effects
     You have, enscheduled briefly, in your hands.

75 **Burgundy**   The King hath heard them, to the which as yet
     There is no answer made.

King Henry   Well then, the peace,
     Which you before so urged, lies in his answer.

hair, send out random shoots. Ryegrass, hemlock, and coarse fumiter grow in her fallow fields; the ploughshare that should uproot them rusts. The level meadow — that formerly grew freckled cowslips, burnet, and green clover — is left unscythed; all unchecked, coarsely luxuriant, seeding itself from neglect; nothing grows but hateful docks, rough thistles, cow parsley, and burdocks, thus losing both its beauty and its usefulness. And all our vineyards, fallow fields, meadows and hedges, prone to degenerate, now grow wild. In the same way, our homes, ourselves and our children have lost (or do not learn from lack of time) the skills that should enhance our country. Instead they grow like savages — as soldiers do who think of nothing else but blood — and take to swearing, aggravation, wearing tatty clothes and everything that seems unnatural. To return all this to its former pleasing state is the reason you have assembled. The purpose of my speech is to seek to know what is preventing gentle peace from banishing these misfortunes, and from blessing us with her former qualities . . .

King Henry   Duke of Burgundy: if you want the peace whose absence causes the problems you have mentioned, you must buy that peace by granting all our just demands; the general principles and particular purposes of which you have listed briefly in the schedule you have in your hands.

Burgundy   The King has heard them. So far he has not replied.

King Henry   Well, then, the peace which you just advocated depends on his answer.

French King   I have but with a cursitory eye
80   O'erglanced the articles. Pleaseth your grace
To appoint some of your council presently
To sit with us once more, with better heed
To re-survey them, we will suddenly
Pass our accept and peremptory answer.

85 **King Henry**   Brother, we shall. Go, Uncle Exeter
And brother Clarence, and you, brother Gloucester;
Warwick and Huntingdon, go with the King,
And take with you free power to ratify,
Augment, or alter, as your wisdoms best
90   Shall see advantageable for our dignity,
Anything in or out of our demands,
And we'll consign thereto. Will you, fair sister,
Go with the princes, or stay here with us?

Queen Isabel   Our gracious brother, I will go with them.
95   Haply a woman's voice may do some good
When articles too nicely urged be stood on.

King Henry   Yet leave our cousin Katherine here with us.
She is our capital demand, comprised
Within the fore-rank of our articles.

100 **Queen Isabel**   She hath good leave.

                    [*Exeunt all but the* **King**, **Katherine**, *and* **Alice**

King Henry   Fair Katherine, and most fair
Will you vouchsafe to teach a soldier terms
Such as will enter at a lady's ear
And plead his love-suit to her gentle heart?

105 **Katherine**   Your majesty shall mock at me. I cannot
speak your England.

King Charles   I have only given the details a cursory glance. If it pleases your grace to appoint some of your Council to confer with us again now, to look over them more carefully, we shall immediately announce our final and absolute answer.

King Henry   Brother, we shall. Go, Uncle Exeter, brother Clarence, brother Gloucester, Warwick and Huntingdon: go with the King. Take with you delegated powers to ratify, add to, or alter anything in – or missing from – our demands, as you in your wisdom think advantageous to our interests. We will then subscribe to it. [*To the* **Queen of France**] Will you, fair sister, go with the princes, or stay here with us?

Queen Isabel   Our gracious brother, I will go with them. Perhaps a woman's voice may do some good when fine details become a stumbling-block.

King Henry   But leave our cousin Katherine here with us. She is our principal demand, and in the forefront of our conditions.

Queen Isabel   She has full permission.

[*The* **King**, **Katherine** and **Alice** *stay, the rest leave*]

King Henry   Fair Katherine, and most beautiful, will you consent to teach a soldier the right words to please a lady, and to plead his case as a suitor to her gentle heart?

Katherine   [*with difficulty, and a strong foreign accent*] Your Majesty shall mock at me. I cannot speak your England.

King Henry   Oh fair Katherine, if you will love me
soundly with your French heart, I will be glad to hear
you confess it brokenly with your English tongue. Do yo
110   like me, Kate?

Katherine   *Pardonnez-moi*, I cannot tell what is 'like me'.

King Henry   An angel is like you, Kate, and you are like
an angel.

Katherine   [*to* **Alice**] *Que dit-il? – que je suis semblable à les*
115   *anges?*

Alice   *Oui, vraiment – sauf votre grace – ainsi dit-il.*

King Henry   I said so, dear Katherine, and I must not
blush to affirm it.

Katherine   *Oh bon Dieu! Les langues des hommes sont pleines*
120   *de tromperies.*

King Henry   What says she, fair one? That the tongues of
men are full of deceits?

Alice   Oui, dat de tongues of de mans is be full of deceits
– dat is de Princess.

125 **King Henry**   The Princess is the better Englishwoman.
I'faith, Kate, my wooing is fit for thy understanding. I
am glad thou canst speak no better English, for if thou
couldst, thou wouldst find me such a plain king that
thou wouldst think I had sold my farm to buy my crown.
130   I know no ways to mince it in love, but directly to say, 'I
love you'; then if you urge me farther than to say, 'Do
you in faith?', I wear out my suit. Give me your answer,
i'faith do, and so clap hands and a bargain. How say
you, lady?

King Henry   Oh, fair Katherine, if you will love me
truly with your French heart, I will be glad to hear
you confess it brokenly in your English accent. Do
you like me, Kate?

Katherine   Forgive me. I cannot tell what is 'like me'.

King Henry   An angel is like you, Kate, and you are
like an angel.

Katherine   [*to* **Alice**] What did he say? That I am like
the angels?

Alice   Yes indeed, Your Grace, that's what he said.

King Henry   I said so, Katherine, and I must not blush
in sticking to it.

Katherine   Oh heavens! Men's tongues are full of idle
flatteries!

King Henry   [*to* **Alice**] What did she say, fair one?
That men's tongues are deceitful?

Alice   Yes; dat de tongues of de mans is be full of
deceits. Dat is what de Princess say.

King Henry   The Princess is all the more an
Englishwoman! Indeed Kate, my wooing is on a
level with your understanding. I'm glad you cannot
speak better English, because if you could, you'd
find me such a plain-speaking King that you'd think
I'd sold my farm to buy my crown. I don't know
how to speak of love in a flowery way, only how to
say bluntly 'I love you'. Then, if you press me
further by saying 'Do you really?', I am silenced.
Give me your answer. Do indeed, and let's shake
hands on a bargain. What do you say, lady?

135 **Katherine**   *Sauf votre honneur*, me understand well.

King Henry   Marry, if you would put me to verses, or to
dance for your sake, Kate, why, you undid me. For the
one I have neither words nor measure, and for the other
I have no strength in measure – yet a reasonable
140   measure in strength. If I could win a lady at leap-frog,
or by vaulting into my saddle with my armour on my
back, under the correction of bragging be it spoken, I
should quickly leap into a wife. Or if I might buffet for
my love, or bound my horse for her favours, I could lay
145   on like a butcher, and sit like a jackanapes, never off.
But before God, Kate, I cannot look greenly, nor gasp
out my eloquence, nor I have no cunning in protestation
– only downright oaths, which I never use till urged, nor
never break for urging. If thou canst love a fellow of this
150   temper, Kate, whose face is not worth sunburning, that
never looks in his glass for love of anything he sees there,
let thine eye be thy cook. I speak to thee plain soldier: if
thou canst love me for this, take me. If not, to say to
thee that I shall die, is true – but for thy love, by the
155   Lord, no. Yet I love thee, too. And while thou livest,
dear Kate, take a fellow of plain and uncoined
constancy, for he perforce must do thee right, because he
hath not the gift to woo in other places. For these fellows
of infinite tongue, that can rhyme themselves into ladies'
160   favours, they do always reason themselves out again.
What! A speaker is but a prater, a rhyme is but a
ballad; a good leg will fall, a straight back will stoop, a
black beard will turn white, a curled pate will grow

Katherine Save your Honour, me understand well.

King Henry Look, if you want me to write poetry, or
dance for your sake, Kate, why, I'm done for. As for
the former, I have neither the vocabulary nor the
metrical ability. And for the latter, I have no
strengths with my feet – though I'm reasonably
good at feats of strength. If I could win a lady at
leapfrog, or by vaulting into my saddle wearing my
armour – subject to correction for boasting – I
should quickly come into a wife. Or if I could box
for my love, or gallop my horse for her favours, I
could go at it like a bruiser and stay mounted like a
monkey, on top all the time. But before God, Kate, I
can't look love-sick, or gasp out my passionate
feelings. I have no skill in solemn declarations of
love, just straightforward vows, which I only make
when urged to do so, and never break whatever the
temptation. If you can love a fellow of this
temperament, Kate, whose face couldn't be uglier
even if it was sunburnt, that never looks in a mirror
out of love for anything he sees there, then may
your eyes turn me into something more palatable. I
speak to you as a plain soldier. If you can love me
for this; take me. If not, to say to you that I'll die is
true – but out of love for you, by the Lord, no! Yet I
do love you. Honestly, Kate, do marry a fellow of
straightforward and genuine loyalty, because he'll
do right by you of necessity, since he hasn't the
ability to woo elsewhere. These fellows with the gift
of the gab, that can rhyme themselves into ladies'
affections, they always reason themselves out
again. What! An orator is only a windbag; a poem
is only a jingle; a good leg will bow; a straight back
will bend; a black beard will turn white; a head of

bald, a fair face will wither, a full eye will wax hollow,
165   but a good heart, Kate, is the sun and the moon – or
rather the sun and not the moon, for it shines bright and
never changes, but keeps his course truly. If thou would
have such a one, take me; and take me, take a soldier;
take a soldier, take a king. And what sayst thou then to
170   my love? Speak, my fair – and fairly, I pray thee.

Katherine   Is it possible dat I sould love de ennemi of
France?

King Henry   No, it is not possible you should love the
enemy of France, Kate. But in loving me, you should
175   love the friend of France, for I love France so well that I
will not part with a village of it; I will have it all mine;
and Kate, when France is mine, and I am yours, then
yours is France, and you are mine.

Katherine   I cannot tell wat is dat.

180 **King Henry**   No Kate? I will tell thee in French – which I
am sure will hang upon my tongue like a new-married
wife about her husband's neck, hardly to be shook off.
*Je quand sur le possesseur de France, et quand vous avez le
possession de moi* – let me see, what then? Saint Denis be
185   my speed! – *donc votre est France, et vous êtes mienne*. It is
as easy for me, Kate, to conquer the kingdom as to
speak so much more French. I shall never move thee in
French, unless it be to laugh at me.

Katherine   *Sauf votre honneur, le francais que vous parlez, il
190   est meilleur que l'anglais lequel je parle.*

curly hair will grow bald; a fine face will crease; a bright eye will sink. But a good heart, Kate, is the sun and the moon – or rather, the sun and not the moon, because it shines bright and never changes, and keeps a true course. If such a one appeals to you, take me. Take me, and take a soldier. Take a soldier, take a King. So what do you say to my love? Speak, my fair one – and fairly, I beg you.

Katherine   Is it possible dat I should love de enemy of France?

King Henry   No. It is not possible you should love the enemy of France, Kate. In loving me, you would love the friend of France, for I love France so well that I will not part with a village of it. I will have it all mine. And Kate, when France is mine, and I am yours, then yours is France, and you are mine.

Katherine   [*the language barrier too great*] I cannot tell what is dat?

King Henry   No, Kate? I'll tell you in French – which I'm sure will cling to my tongue like a newlywed around her husband's neck, hardly to be disengaged. When I possess France, and when you have the possession of me – let me see what then? St Denis, [*the patron saint of France*] come to my aid! Therefore, yours is France and you are mine. It's as easy for me, Kate, to conquer the kingdom as it is to speak any more French. I shall never persuade you in the French language, unless it be to laugh at me!

Katherine   Save Your Honour, the French which you speak is better than the English with which I speak.

King Henry No, faith, is't not, Kate. But thy speaking of my tongue, and I thine, most truly-falsely, must needs be granted to be much at one. But Kate, dost thou understand thus much English? Canst thou love me?

195 **Katherine** I cannot tell.

King Henry Can any of your neighbours tell, Kate? I'll ask them. Come, I know thou lovest me, and at night when you come into your closet you'll question this gentlewoman about me, and I know, Kate, you will to
200 her disprayse those parts in me that you love with your heart. But good Kate, mock me mercifully – the rather, gentle princess, because I love thee cruelly. If ever thou be'st mine, Kate – as I have a saving faith within me tells me thou shalt – I get thee with scambling, and thou
205 must therefore needs prove a good soldier-breeder. Shall not thou and I, between Saint Denis and Saint George, compound a boy, half-French half-English, that shall go to Constantinople and take the Turk by the beard? Shall we not? What sayst thou, my fair flower-de-luce?

210 **Katherine** I do not know dat.

King Henry No, 'tis hereafter to know, but now to promise. Do but now promise, Kate, you will endeavour for your French part of such a boy, and for my English moiety take the word of a king and a bachelor. How
215 answer you, *la plus belle Katherine du monde, mon tres chère et divine déesse?*

256

King Henry   No, indeed it isn't, Kate. But your speaking my language and I yours in a garbled fashion must assuredly be very similar. But Kate, do you understand this much English? Can you love me?

Katherine   I cannot tell.

King Henry   Can any of your neighbours tell, Kate? I'll ask them. Come, I know you love me, and tonight when you go to your bedroom you will question this gentlewoman about me; and I know, Kate, you will criticise those things about me that you love with all your heart. But good Kate, mock me mercifully – if only, gentle princess, because I love you extremely. If you are ever to be mine, Kate – and I have a strong feeling inside me that tells me that you shall – I'll win you only after a tussle, so you ought to be a good mother of soldiers. Shall not you and I, between our two patron saints, conceive a boy – half French, half English – who will go to Constantinople and tackle the Turks there? [*Henry VI, their son, did that very thing*] Shall we not? What do you say, my beautiful lily flower? [*The emblem of the French monarchy*]

Katherine   I do not know dat.

King Henry   No, later comes the experience; now is the time to promise. Just promise now, Kate, that you'll try your best for the French part of such a boy; and for my English half – take the word of a king and a bachelor. What's your answer, the most beautiful Katherine in the world, my very dear and divine goddess?

Katherine   Your majesty 'ave *fausse* French enough to deceive de most *sage demoiselle* dat is *en France*.

King Henry   Now fie upon my false French! By mine
220   honour, in true English, I love thee Kate. By which
honour I dare not swear thou lovest me, yet my blood
begins to flatter me that thou dost, notwithstanding the
poor and untempering effect of my visage. Now beshrew
my father's ambition! He was thinking of civil wars
225   when he got me; therefore was I created with a stubborn
outside, with an aspect of iron, that when I come to woo
ladies I fright them. But in faith, Kate, the elder I wax
the better I shall appear. My comfort is that old age,
that ill layer-up of beauty, can do no more spoil upon
230   my face. Thou hast me, if thou hast me, at the worst,
and thou shalt wear me, if thou wear me, better and
better; and therefore tell me, most fair Katherine, will
you have me? Put off your maiden blushes, avouch the
thoughts of your heart with the looks of an empress, take
235   me by the hand and say, 'Harry of England, I am thine'
– which word thou shalt no sooner bless mine ear withal,
but I will tell thee aloud, 'England is thine, Ireland is
thine, France is thine, and Henry Plantagenet is thine' –
who, though I speak it before his face, if he be not fellow
240   with the best king, thou shalt find the best king of good
fellows. Come, your answer in broken music – for thy
voice is music and thy English broken. Therefore, queen
of all, Katherine, break thy mind to me in broken
English: wilt thou have me?

Katherine   Your Majesty 'ave enough bad French to deceive de most wise young lady dat is in France.

King Henry   To blazes with my bad French! By my honour, in good English, I love you Kate. By that same honour, I dare not swear that you love me; yet something inside me begins to flatter me that you do, notwithstanding the poor and off-putting effect of my looks. Curse my father's ambition! He was thinking of civil wars when I was conceived; therefore I was born looking tough, with a grim facial expression, so that when I come courting ladies, I frighten them. Actually, Kate, the older I get the better I shall look. My comfort is that old age, that wrinkler of beauty, cannot do my face any further harm. You have me – if you'll have me – at my worst; and you shall take to me – if you take to me – better and better. Therefore, tell me most beautiful Katherine – will you have me? Put away your maidenly blushes; align the thoughts of your heart with the looks of an empress; take me by the hand and say 'Harry of England, I am yours'. No sooner shall you bless my ear with those words, but I'll tell you, aloud, 'England is yours; Ireland is yours; France is yours; and Henry Plantagenet is yours'. And if he – though I say it to his face – if he is not actually the best king, it's because 'the best king' [*according to the old English proverb*] is 'the King of Good Fellows'. [*He married the Queen of Beggars*] Come, give me your answer in broken music [*he means music that is 'broken up', or 'arranged' in parts*]: because your voice is music and your English is broken. Therefore, queen of all, Katherine, break your silence to me in broken English. Will you have me?

245 **Katherine**   Dat is as it shall please *de roi mon père*.

King Henry   Nay, it will please him well, Kate. It shall please him, Kate.

Katherine   Den it shall also content me.

King Henry   Upon that I kiss your hand, and I call you
250   my queen.

Katherine   *Laissez mon seigneur, laissez, laissez! Ma foi, je ne veux point que vous abaissiez votre grandeur en baisant la main d'une de votre seigneurie indigne serviteur. Excusez-moi je vous supplie, mon très-puissant seigneur.*

255 **King Henry**   Then I will kiss your lips, Kate.

Katherine   *Les dames et demoiselles pour être baisées devant leurs noces, il n'est pas la coutume de France.*

King Henry   [*to* **Alice**] Madam my interpreter, what says she?

260 **Alice**   Dat it is not be de *façon pour les ladies* of France – I cannot tell vat is *baiser* en Anglish–

King Henry   To kiss.

Alice   Your majesty *entendre bettre que moi.*

King Henry   It is not a fashion for the maids in France to
265   kiss before they are married, would she say?

Alice   *Oui, vraiment.*

King Henry   Oh Kate, nice customs curtsy to great kings. Dear Kate, you and I cannot be confined within the weak list of a country's fashion. We are the makers of
270   manners, Kate, and the liberty that follows our places

Katherine   Dat is as it shall please de King my father.

King Henry   [*grimly confident*] It will please him greatly, Kate. It will please him, Kate.

Katherine   Den it shall also content me.

King Henry   Upon that, I kiss your hand and I call you my queen. [*He raises her hand to his lips*]

Katherine   [*pulling it away sharply*] Stop, stop, my lord, stop, stop! My goodness, I would not have you lower yourself by kissing the hand of one of Your Majesty's humble servants. Excuse me, I beg you, my thrice-powerful lord.

King Henry   Then I will kiss your lips, Kate.

Katherine   For ladies and gentlemen to kiss before their marriage is not the French custom.

King Henry   [*to* **Alice**] Madam my interpreter: what does she say?

Alice   Dat it is not be the fashion for the ladies of France – I cannot tell what is 'baiser' in Anglish.

King Henry   To kiss . . .

Alice   Your Majesty understands better than I.

King Henry   It is not the fashion for the young ladies in France to kiss before they are married: is that what she says?

Alice   Yes, indeed.

King Henry   Oh, Kate: prim and proper customs bow before great kings. Dear Kate, you and I cannot be held prisoner by a country's fashions. We are the makers of etiquette, Kate, and the latitude that goes

stops the mouth of all find-faults, as I will do yours, for
upholding the nice fashion of your country in denying m‹
a kiss. Therefore, patiently and yielding. [*He kisses her*]
You have witchcraft in your lips, Kate. There is more
275 eloquence in a sugar touch of them than in the tongues
of the French Council, and they should sooner persuade
Harry of England than a general petition of monarchs.
Here comes your father.

[*Enter the* **French King,** *his* **Queen, Burgundy** *and*
Lords]

Burgundy   God save your majesty. My royal cousin, teach
280 you our princess English?

King Henry   I would have her learn, my fair cousin, how
perfectly I love her, and that is good English.

Burgundy   Is she not apt?

King Henry   Our tongue is rough, coz, and my condition
285 is not smooth, so that having neither the voice nor the
heart of flattery about me I cannot so conjure up the
spirit of love in her that he will appear in his true
likeness.

Burgundy   Pardon the frankness of my mirth, if I answer
290 you for that. If you would conjure in her, you must
make a circle; if conjure up love in her in his true
likeness, he must appear naked and blind. Can you
blame her then, being a maid yet rosed over with the
virgin crimson of modesty, if she deny the appearance of
295 a naked blind boy in her naked seeing self? It were, my
lord, a hard condition for a maid to consign to.

with our rank shuts the mouths of all spoil-sports as I shall do yours, for upholding the priggish fashion of your country in denying me a kiss. Therefore, consentingly and yielding . . . [*He kisses her*] There is magic in your lips, Kate. There is more eloquence in the sweet touch of them than in the speeches of the French Council, and they would be more influential with Harry of England than a delegation of monarchs. Here comes your father.

[**King Charles**, **Queen Isabel**, *the* **Duke of Burgundy** *and the French and English lords enter, looking pleased*]

Burgundy   God save Your Majesty. My royal cousin: did you teach our princess English?

King Henry   I wanted her to learn, dear cousin, how perfectly I love her, and that is good English!

Burgundy   Isn't she raring to go?

King Henry   Our language is rough, cousin, and I am not smooth-tongued by nature. So having neither the words nor the temperament for flattery in me, I cannot raise the spirit of love in her enough for it to seem like the real thing.

Burgundy   Forgive the indelicacy of my wit if I take you up on that. If you wish to rise up in her, you must enter the magic circle; and to rise 'like the real thing', your love must be naked and blind, like Cupid. Can you blame her then, since she is still a blushing virgin, if she declines to let a naked blind boy intrude into her exposed self? It would be, my lord, a stiff proposition for a young lady to agree to.

King Henry   Yet they do wink and yield, as love is blind
and enforces.

Burgundy   They are then excused, my lord, when they see
300   not what they do.

King Henry   Then, good my lord, teach your cousin to
consent winking.

Burgundy   I will wink on her to consent, my lord, if you
will teach her to know my meaning. For maids, well
305   summered and warm kept, are like flies at Bartholomew-
tide: blind, though they have their eyes. And then they
will endure handling, which before would not abide
looking on.

King Henry   This moral ties me over to time and a hot
310   summer, and so I shall catch the fly, your cousin, in the
latter end, and she must be blind too.

Burgundy   As love is, my lord, before it loves.

King Henry   It is so. And you may, some of you, thank
love for my blindness, who cannot see many a fair
315   French city for one fair French maid that stands in my
way.

French King   Yes, my lord, you see them perspectively,
the cities turned into a maid – for they are all girdled
with maiden walls that war hath never entered.

320 **King Henry**   Shall Kate be my wife?

French King   So please you.

King Henry   Nevertheless, maidens close their eyes and submit, because love is wilful and has its way regardless.

Burgundy   They are then forgiven, my lord, when they cannot see what they are doing.

King Henry   Well then, good my lord, teach your cousin to turn a blind eye . . .

Burgundy   I will tip her the wink to consent, my lord, if you will teach her to understand what I'm saying. Because young ladies who are well-brought up and comfortably off are like flies in late August: too dozy to see, though they are not blind. Then you can do what you will with them, though before they wouldn't even let you look at them.

King Henry   This theory commits me to a long wait and a hot summer, so I shall eventually catch the fly – your cousin – from behind! And she must have her eyes closed, too!

Burgundy   Like love, my lord, before it awakes . . .

King Henry   Just so. And you can thank love, some of you, for my own blindness, in that one beautiful French maiden blocks out the sight of many a fine French city.

King Charles   Yes, my lord, you see them distortedly – cities in the form of a young woman. They are all encircled by virginal walls that have never been entered by war.

King Henry   Shall Kate be my wife?

King Charles   If you so wish.

King Henry   I am content, so the maiden cities you talk o:
may wait on her: so the maid that stood in the way for
my wish shall show me the way to my will.

325 **French King**   We have consented to all terms of reason.

King Henry   Is't so, my lords of England?

Westmorland   The King hath granted every article:
His daughter first, and then in sequel all,
According to their firm proposed natures.

330 **Exeter**   Only he hath not yet subscribed this: where your
majesty demands that the King of France, having any
occasion to write for matter of grant, shall name your
highness in this form and with this addition: in French,
Notre très cher fils Henri, Roi d'Angleterre, Heritier de
335 France, and thus in Latin, Praeclarissimus filius noster
Henricus, Rex Angliae et Haeres Franciae.

French King   Nor this I have not, brother, so denied,
But your request shall make me let it pass.

King Henry   I pray you then, in love and dear alliance,
340 Let that one article rank with the rest,
And thereupon give me your daughter.

French King   Take her, fair son, and from her blood raise
up
Issue to me, that the contending kingdoms
345 Of France and England, whose very shores look pale
With envy of each other's happiness,
May cease their hatred, and this dear conjunction
Plant neighbourhood and Christian-like accord
In their sweet bosoms, that never war advance
350 His bleeding sword 'twixt England and fair France.

King Henry   I am happy, provided the maiden cities of which you speak go with her. That way, the maid that stood in the way of my aims shall help me achieve my objectives.

King Charles   We have agreed to all reasonable terms . . .

King Henry   Is that so, my lords of England?

Westmorland   The King has granted everything: first his daughter, then all the succeeding clauses, in precise detail.

Exeter   Except that he has not yet agreed to the part where Your Majesty demands that the King of France, whenever he should have reason to write to you over a matter concerning gifts of land or conferment of titles, shall address your highness in this style and rank: in French, 'Our most dear son Henry, King of England, heir to France' and likewise in Latin 'Praeclarissimus filius noster Henricus, Rex Angliae et Haeres Franciae'.

King Charles   I'm not so adamant, brother, that I wouldn't yield if you requested me.

King Henry   I ask you, then, in love and valued friendship: let that one clause remain with the rest, and then grant me your daughter.

King Charles   Take her, dear son, and father me children by her, so that the rival kingdoms of France and England, both of whose shores are chalky white with envy of each other's happiness, will cease their hatred, and this dear marriage instil neighbourliness and Christian-like harmony in their hearts, to end all bloody wars between England and fair France.

Lords Amen!

King Henry Now welcome, Kate, and bear me witness all
That here I kiss her as my sovereign Queen.

[*Flourish*]

Queen Isabel God, the best maker of all marriages,
355   Combine your hearts in one, your realms in one.
As man and wife, being two, are one in love,
So be there 'twixt your kingdoms such a spousal
That never may ill office or fell jealousy,
Which troubles oft the bed of blessed marriage,
360   Thrust in between the paction of these kingdoms
To make divorce of their incorporate league;
That English may as French, French Englishmen,
Receive each other, God speak this 'Amen'.

Lords Amen!

365 **King Henry** Prepare we for our marriage. On which day,
My lord of Burgundy, we'll take your oath,
And all the peers', for surety of our leagues.
Then shall I swear to Kate, and you to me,
And may our oaths well kept and prosp'rous be.

[*Sennet. Exeunt*]

Lords   Amen.

King Henry   Now welcome, Kate! Everyone bear witness that I kiss her here as my sovereign Queen.

[*Trumpets sound as the* **King** *and his bride-to-be embrace*]

Queen Isabel   God, the best maker of all marriages, unite your hearts as one, and your realms as one. Just as man and wife, though two people, are one in terms of love, so may there be such a marriage between your kingdoms that neither wrong-doing nor cruel jealousy (which often trouble the blessed marriage-bed) may break the bond between these kingdoms, causing them to be divorced. That the English may regard themselves as French and vice versa, God say 'Amen'.

Lords   Amen.

King Henry   Let us prepare for our marriage. On that day, my lord of Burgundy, we'll accept your oath of fidelity, and that of all the peers, to ratify our alliance. Then I shall pledge myself to Kate, and you to me; and may our oaths be well kept and lead to prosperity.

[*Trumpets sound. Everyone leaves in state*]

Epilogue

Enter **Chorus**

Chorus   Thus far with rough and all-unable pen
    Our bending author hath pursued the story,
In little room confining mighty men,
    Mangling by starts the full course of their glory.
5 Small time, but in that small most greatly lived
    This star of England. Fortune made his sword,
By which the world's best garden he achieved,
    And of it left his son imperial lord.
Henry the Sixth, in infant bands crowned king.
10   Of France and England, did this king succeed,
Whose state so many had the managing
    That they lost France and made his England bleed,
Which oft our stage hath shown – and, for their sake,
In your fair minds let this acceptance take.

                                 [*Exit*

Epilogue

The **Announcer** *enters.*

Announcer   So far, then, has our studious author
taken the story, with his rough and selective pen;
confining men of might into a small space [*he
gestures towards the stage*] and distorting the full
history of their glorious exploits by selecting only
some of them. Short was his lifetime [*Henry died
aged 35*] but in that shortness this star of England
lived in greatness. His sword was forged for war,
and with it he achieved the world's finest realm,
leaving his son the imperial monarch of it. Henry
the Sixth, crowned when only a baby succeeded
this King. So many politicians were the power
behind the throne that they lost France, and brought
internal strife to England, as many plays in this
theatre have shown. [*He is referring to
Shakespeare's three plays about Henry VI and their
production at the Globe Theatre*] These considered,
may this one be acceptable to your fair minds.

[*He bows and leaves*]

271

Activities

Characters

Search the text (either the original or the modern version) to find answers to the following questions. They will help you to form personal opinions about the major characters in the play. Record any relevant quotations in Shakespeare's own words.

Henry

1 a In *Act 1 Scene 1*, the King's character is described in glowing terms by the two clerics. What do we learn about:

    i his past history and former companions

    ii his reformation

    iii his talents in divinity, diplomacy, military strategy, politics, and discourse?

  b What can we deduce are the necessary virtues of an ideal Christian king?

  c Consider the danger to the Church described by the Archbishop, and his proposed solution.

    i Is there a touch of irony in what the prelates say about Henry's piety?

    ii If so, what does this tell us about Henry's true character?

2 Henry's claim to the French throne is expounded at great length in *Act 1 Scene 2*.

  a What could be the motives of a newly-crowned king in fighting a foreign war when his father's reign has been a troubled one at home?

   b Does he embark on it with the fulsome support of
   the Church and his nobles?

   c What is the final straw that makes war with France
   a patriotic duty, and how does Henry's handling of
   it do him credit?

3 By *Act 2 Scene 2*, Henry is on his way to France and
faced with treachery.

   a Say what qualities of character are shown in his
   handling of the case of 'the man . . . that railed
   against our person'.

   b Say what qualities are shown in his handling of the
   'English monsters', Cambridge, Scroop and Grey.

4 The Chorus takes us swiftly to the gates of besieged
Harfleur. In the Prologue and *Act 3 Scene 1*:

   a How do we know that Henry's determination to fight
   a war in France cannot be bought off?

   b How does the King inspire his troops by means of
     i appeals to manliness
     ii references to ancestry and honour
     iii calls to patriotism?

5 **a** In his address to the Governor of Harfleur, how does
   Henry show:
     i his ruthlessness when circumstances require it
     ii his dislike of unnecessary cruelty
     iii his merciful qualities?

   b How are all three demonstrated again in *Act 3 Scene
   6*, after the battle for the bridge in Picardy?

6 The Chorus describes Henry on the eve of the Battle of
Agincourt: 'a little touch of Harry in the night'. What
do we learn about:

   a his demeanour

   b his looks

   c his effect on the English troops?

7 Wearing the cloak of Sir Thomas Erpingham, Henry

meets a cross-section of his fighting men in *Act 4
Scene 1*.

a First he meets Pistol. Illustrate from their dialogue:
   i Henry's good humour
   ii Henry's tolerance
   iii Henry's adroitness in concealing his identity
   while telling the truth.

b After hearing Fluellen chide Gower for speaking too
loudly, Henry meets three ordinary soldiers: Bates,
Court and Williams.
   i From Henry's speech 'The King is but a man'
   (*lines 101–112*) show how he reveals that he has
   not lost the common touch in spite of his regal
   status.
   ii What is Henry's answer to the charge that the
   King is ultimately responsible if he fights an
   unjust war?
   iii How near to anger is Henry, faced with the
   frank observations of Michael Williams?
   iv What is the outcome of their quarrel?
   v What is the 'hard condition' of which Henry
   complains in his soliloquy, and what are his
   feelings about 'ceremony'?
   vi How do we know that on the eve of battle his
   thoughts and fears go back to troubles of his
   father's making?

8 Henry excels at rallying his men and inspiring them
with his patriotic fervour. In *Act 4 Scene 3* he makes
two memorable speeches.

a In the first 'What's he that wishes so?', show how he
   i overcomes fears that the English army is too
   small
   ii argues the case for honour
   iii makes out the case for pride.

b In the second 'I pray thee bear my former answer
back' (*lines 97–132*)

    i Illustrate Henry's refusal to be intimidated
    ii Demonstrate that he does not lose his sense of
    reality
    iii Show how he turns his army's ragged
    appearance into a positive virtue.

9 The Battle of Agincourt rages over several scenes. In
  Act 4 Scene 6
    i What line suggests Henry has a tender heart?
    ii What line shows him at his most cold-blooded?

10 In *Act 4 Scene 7* Gower gives an explanation for the
   slaughter of the French prisoners.
   a What is it?
   b Does this show Henry in a different light?
   c Can you offer any explanation for the apparent
     contradiction?

11 Montjoy the Herald concedes defeat.
   a   i Whose is the victory, according to Henry?
      ii After naming the battle, what is the first thing
         Henry does?
     iii What is the second?
   b What light relief (after the tension of Battle) does
     this lead to, and
   c What does it tell us about Henry's longstanding
     rapport with ordinary men?

12 A five-year gap of time separates Act 4 from Act 5; the
   Chorus fills in some of the details.
   a What kind of reception did Henry receive on landing
     in England from France?
   b What kind of reception did he receive in London?
   c What was remarkable about his journey through
     Blackheath?
   d What kept Henry in England?
   e Whose intervention led him to return to France?

13 a At the palace of King Charles, Henry's diplomats negotiate a peace while the King woos Katherine, the French king's daughter.

      i Why does Henry say he needs instruction in the art of courtship?

      ii What kind of a king does he says he is?

      iii What kind of skills does he say he has?

      iv What kind of skills does he say he lacks?

      vi What does he admit about his looks?

      vii What is his explanation for them, and for his personality?

   b How do we know from what Henry says that he has no need to ask for King Charles's consent to their marriage?

14 a The final stage of the courtship is marked with kisses.

      i Why does Katherine protest when Henry kisses her hand?

      ii Why does she protest when he offers to kiss her lips?

      iii What phrase of Henry's explains why the betrothal is sealed in the English fashion?

   b What final concession do the French make to ensure peace between the two kingdoms?

The English Nobles

1 The Duke of Exeter. Like all the minor characters in this play dominated by a hero king, the Duke's role is purely functional. What task does he perform:

   a In *Act 1 Scene 2*?

   b In *Act 2 Scene 2*?

   c In *Act 2 Scene 4*?

   d In *Act 3 Scene 3*?

   e In Picardy?

   f At the Battle of Agincourt?

   g At the peace conference?

2 The Dukes of York, Westmorland, Bedford, Gloucester and Warwick

   a Which Noble warns Henry about the danger of a Scots invasion?

   b Which Noble thinks Henry is taking a risk in trusting the traitors as far as Southampton?

   c Which Noble is in charge of the mines at Harfleur?

   d Which Noble tells Henry he is in great danger, on the eve of the battle of Agincourt?

   e Which Noble summons Henry to the battle?

   f Which Noble is rebuked for wishing the English army was bigger?

   g Which Noble requests to be leader of the vanguard?

   h Whose dying words were 'Commend my service to my sovereign'?

The French Nobles King Charles; the Dauphin; Burgundy; Orleans; Britaine; The Constable; Rambures, Grandpré; Montjoy the Herald

   a Who sends Henry 'this tun of treasure', and what does it contain?

   b Which five are sent by King Charles to strengthen the French defences in anticipation of the English invasion?

   c Who tells the Dauphin he is mistaken about Harry's character?

   d Who wants more time to consider Henry's pre-invasion proposals?

   e Who is not ready to give Harfleur the assistance needed to raise the seige?

   f Who will sell his dukedom and buy 'a slobbery and a dirty farm' if the English were unchallenged?

    g Who describes the English climate as 'foggy, raw and dull'?

    h Who wishes the English army were bigger?

    i Who is praised for doing his office fairly?

    j Who claims to have the best armour in the world?

    k Whose horse is 'the prince of palfreys'?

    l Who has stars upon his armour?

    m Who tries to place a bet on the number of prisoners he will take?

    n Who measures the ground between the two armies at Agincourt?

    o Who chooses a short life in preference to one of shame?

    p Which other Nobles die at Agincourt?

    q Who master-minds the peace conference?

Katherine

1   Katherine does not appear until *Act 3 Scene 4*, where she is learning English.

    a How many words does she learn altogether?

    b Why do some of the words shock her?

2   When she appears again (historically, five years later) she has made considerable progress.

    a How do we know she sometimes:

       i guesses the meaning of words and

       ii understands what really matters?

    b How do we know she is:

       i patriotic

       ii obedient to her father's wishes

       iii not averse to flattery

       iv well brought up

       v submissive?

3   How do we know the marriage produced an heir?

The Low-life Characters Nym; Bardolph; Pistol; Hostess

Shakespearian audiences were familiar with the three cowardly rogues and the keeper of the Boar's Head Tavern, Eastcheap, from the earlier history plays, *Henry IV Parts One* and *Two*.

1 They first appear in *Act 2 Scene 1*
   a Which has a cryptic manner of speech? Give examples.
   b Which is the one whose fiery face is the subject of mockery?
   c Which of the three rogues talks like a ham actor? Find some typical examples.
   d How does the Hostess:
      i mis-use words with comical effect?
      ii unconsciously utter phrases with bawdy double-meanings?
   e Who was first engaged to the Hostess?
   f Who became the Hostess's husband?
   g Give examples of how they squabble and swear at each other.

2 In their next appearance in *Act 2 Scene 3*, they are sad and subdued. Their old friend Falstaff has died of a broken heart, having been rejected by the new king after a long friendship.
   a Explain the poignancy of the Hostess's description of Falstaff's end.
   b From their observations and reminiscences, what sort of a man was Falstaff?
   c How do the Eastcheap rogues reveal their individual characters in the way they react to Falstaff's death?
   d Is patriotism their reason for joining the army in France?

3 At Harfleur, the three men and the Boy take part in the seige.
   a Are there any signs of gallantry amongst them? Describe their behaviour.
   b Study what the Boy says of them. Is he right in deciding to look for better employment?

4 Bardolph is in serious trouble by *Act 3 Scene 6*.
   a What offence has he committed?
   b How does Pistol try to help him, and what response does he get?

5 Pistol meets the King in *Act 4 Scene 1*.
   a How does Pistol boast outrageously?
   b How is he presumptuous?
   c How is he aggressive?
   d Does he deserve the King's tolerant good-humour?

6 Pistol takes a French prisoner in *Act 4 Scene 4*.
   a Explain the comic consequences of the language barrier.
   b In *Act 5 Scene 1* how does Fluellen accomplish the total humiliation of the cowardly braggart?
   c What news is revealed which confirms that 'Dame Fortune has played the housewife' with the last remaining survivor of the King's Eastcheap acquaintances?

The Army Captains Fluellen; Gower; MacMorris; Jamy

That the war against France should be won by Welsh, English, Irish and Scots soldiers under a united banner would have been of special significance to Shakespeare's audiences after 1603 when James VI of Scotland became James I of England, thus bringing the whole of the British Isles under one king. It may be that *Act 3 Scene 2* was added to the play at this time.

1 Show from the scene in which they all appear (*Act 3 Scene 2*) that:
   a Fluellen has fixed ideas about how war should be fought. What are they?
   b Fluellen is intolerant of those whose theories differ from his. Who is his main target for abuse?
   c Fluellen likes a good argument. Does he get one?
   d Fluellen has problems with what to him is a second language. Give examples.

2 In the same scene
   a MacMorris makes his only appearance in the play. What do we learn of:
      i his dedication to gunpowder and warfare
      ii his impatience
      iii his national sensitivity?
   b What do we learn about Captain Jamy's soldiership and his liking for a good debate?

3 a Fluellen reappears in *Act 3 Scene 6*, at the English camp in Picardy. Surprisingly, he compares Pistol's behaviour at the bridge with the bravery of Mark Antony.
      i What other classical models are cited by Fluellen in the play, and which one is likely to be the source of most amusement to an English audience?
      ii Pistol is wordy, but Fluellen can hold his own. Give examples of the latter's verbosity, in this scene and elsewhere.
      iii What, ultimately, is the criterion by which Fluellen comes to a judgement on the field of battle?
   b Explain Gower's role in the scene, and say what it tells you of his character.

4 There is an amusing Gower-Fluellen interlude in *Act 4 Scene 1*. Explain:

   a why it is comic

   b why the King's comment is deserved, and

   c why producers often make Fluellen shout his last line?

5 They appear together again in *Act 4 Scene 7*.

   a What seems to worry Fluellen most about the massacre of the boys?

   b What is absurd about Fluellen's case for comparing King Henry with Alexander the Great?

   c How do we know Fluellen likes to have his say?

   d Find some amusing examples of how Fluellen says it.

   e Find some amusing examples of Fluellen's Welsh patriotism.

6 **a** Explain how Fluellen, 'touched with choler, hot as gunpowder', is sent on the King's mission to deal with Williams (*Act 4 Scene 8*).

   b Describe how 'a Welsh correction' teaches Pistol 'a good English condition' in *Act 5 Scene 1*.

   c In both cases:

     i Show how Fluellen's inability to 'speak English in the native garb' is evident in his use of synonyms, strange grammatical forms, and repetitions.

     ii Illustrate the comic consequences of his unfailing politeness and eccentricity.

The Common Soldiers John Bates; Alexander Court; Michael Williams

Court is the quiet one; Bates would prefer to be 'in the Thames up to the neck' rather than in France on the eve of a battle, and Williams articulates the plight of the simple

man involved in wars beyond his knowledge and
understanding.

1 a Find two examples of the lukewarm involvement of
      Bates.
   b Find an example of his humility.
   c Find an example of his bravery.
   d Find an example of his practical common sense.

2 a Show that Williams is aware he is a conscripted
      soldier: 'his not to reason why, his but to do and
      die'.
   b Illustrate his shrewd understanding of war stripped
      of its heroics.
   c Illustrate his shrewd understanding of politics in high
      places.
   d Adjudicate between Williams and the King on the
      subject of the 'foolish saying'. In your opinion, who
      is right?

3 The Williams episode comes to a head in *Act 4 Scenes 7
   and 8*.
   a Give examples of Williams' 'blunt bearing', and
      show how Fluellen's advice to the King overcomes
      the class problem in the working-out of the dispute.
   b Is the King's practical joke made plausible because
      we know he has mixed in humble circles in his
      youth?
   c What is Williams' case for escaping execution?
   d How is the manner of his expressing it in keeping
      with his character?
   e How is his response to Fluellen's gift also indicative
      of his character?

Textual questions

Read the original Shakespeare and (if necessary) the modern transcription to gain an understanding of the speeches and extracts below. Then concentrate entirely on the original in answering the questions.

1 *Oh for a Muse of fire . . . (Prologue to Act 1)*
   a What is the dramatic advantage of beginning the play with an exclamation?
   b What is the patriotic advantage of referring to the King as 'Harry'?
   c Explain the effectiveness of the image of the hounds.
   d The Chorus begs the pardon of his audience.
      i What words does he use in avoiding the term 'theatre'?
      ii What words suggest the humility of the actors?
      iii Why does he call them 'ciphers in this great account'?
   e What is his way of indicating that large things can be scaled down?
   f The Chorus asks the audience to 'piece out our imperfections with your thoughts'. What specific examples does he give?
   g What does he say about the time-scale of the play?
   h i What is the advantage of concluding the Prologue with a rhyming couplet?
      ii Check whether this is standard throughout the play.
      iii Consider what action by the Chorus would be appropriate as he utters his final words.

2 *We are glad the Dauphin is so pleasant with us (Act I Scene 2 (lines 269–309))*

   a Show how the King opens his speech with politeness and irony.

   b How does he use the game of tennis as a metaphor for war?

   c What effective use does he make of his confession about a mis-spent youth?

   d Explain the image of 'light' and comment on its relationship to the phrase 'plodded like a man '.

   e Show how he plays upon the word 'mock' to turn it against the Dauphin and his 'merry message'.

   f Why do you think the speech ends with a rhyming couplet?

3 *Now all the youth of England are on fire (Prologue to Act 2)*

   a Explain how the clothing metaphor in line 2 contrasts with the harsh fact of war in line 3.

   b The critic Caroline Spurgeon has pointed out that a theme word in *Henry V* is 'flight', suggesting the swift movement of birds. Where is this borne out here?

   c What is the Chorus's flattering metaphor for King Henry?

   d How does the Chorus use personification to convey a sense of the King's formidable strength?

   e How does he use apostrophe to convey a sense of dismay?

   f How does the use of a pun grimly emphasise the iniquity of the three traitors?

   g How does he continue the theme, begun in the prologue to Act 1, of imagination overcoming obstacles like distance?

   h Explain his joke about the sea-crossing.

4 *Nay, sure, he's not in hell. He's in Arthur's bosom (Act 2 Scene 3 lines 9–25)*

  a In what circumstances does Shakespeare normally use prose?

  b By 'Arthur's bosom', the Hostess means 'Abraham's bosom', or heaven; this is one of her many verbal errors. Why, in the circumstances, is this a passage for tears rather than laughter?

  c   i How does humour and pathos intermix in the section where the Hostess uses direct speech?

      ii The Hostess is notorious for her innocent use of words with two meanings, one being bawdy. In Elizabethan times, 'stone' could mean 'testicle'. Is this another case where the audience wants to laugh and cry at the same time?

5 *Thus with imagined wing our swift scene flies (Prologue to Act 3)*

  a Show how the imagery of flight noted in question **3b** is in evidence here.

  b   i How does the Chorus convey the busyness of a fleet setting sail and crossing the English channel?

      ii Explain how the audience is to keep up with the ships on their way to Harfleur.

  c Which words keep up the excitement and pace of the journey?

  d   i Which words convey the menace of the artillery beseiging Harfleur?

      ii How does the movement of the verse vividly convey the effect of the 'nimble gunner's' linstock?

6 *Once more unto the breach, dear friends, once more (Act 3 Scene 1 (lines 1–35))*

  a This is one of Shakespeare's best known set

speeches. How does the use of monosyllables give it its famous initial impact?

b What use is made of animal imagery?

c Which words help the passage to gather pace?

d Which words convey the savagery and harshness of war?

e Which words suggest tenseness, and the extremity of physical effort?

f Which appeal to patriotism; ancestry; pride?

g How does he appeal to English yeomen with a touch of wit?

h How does the movement of the verse follow a 'Ready, steady, go!' pattern?

7 *Now entertain conjecture of a time (Prologue to Act 4)*

a In contrast with the explosive start of the Chorus's first speech in the play, this prologue begins quietly. Find the words which convey the muffled silence of the middle of the night.

b What sounds are registered up to 3 a.m.?

c What two forms of light are mentioned in the passage?

d Why are the soldiers' faces 'umbered'?

e Examine the imagery used to convey the French nobles' feeling that dawn is slow in coming.

f Why do the English troops look like ghosts?

g How does Henry introduce warmth and light to the 'poor condemned English'?

h Comment on the meaning and effectiveness of 'A little touch of Harry in the night'.

i Identify another example of 'flight'.

j Explain the embarrassment of the Chorus as expressed in the last five lines.

8 *But if the cause be not good (Act 4 Scene 1 (lines 133–144))*

a Williams' prose speech is in marked contrast to the heroic poetry of the King and the Chorus, and so is

Activities

its content. To what extent is this due to his
imaginative way of visualising disembodied limbs
rather than, say, ranks of soldiers?
b How does his mundane 'chopped off in a battle'
sustain the stark picture he is conveying?
c How is the horrific reality of war further conveyed in
the cries of the dead?
d Conventionally, all men die well that die in battle.
(Find an example in *Act 4 Scene 6*). What is
Williams' reason for disputing this, and upon whom
does the responsibility lie?

9 *What's he that wishes so? (Act 4 Scene 3 (lines 22–31))*
a What is the effect of Henry's use of expletives, three
in all?
b What is the effect of his use of words of one syllable?
c What is the effect of the repetition of 'this day'?
d What is the effect of the catalogue of noble names?
e 'Remembered' is a word of four syllables: those that
follow are short and simple. Account for their
memorable qualities.
f How many times does Henry mention 'Crispian',
and why is it dramatically effective to end the last
line with a variant of it?

10 *Vouchsafe to those who have not read the story (Prologue to
Act 5)*
a In what way does the Chorus repeat his apology for
the shortcomings of a stage play?
b Find another example of the 'flight' imagery.
c Trace the way in which the audience is taken from
location to location.
d Which line is a particularly vivid reference to the
imagination?
e Which lines have a contemporary reference which
enables scholars to date the play?

288

Examination questions and coursework assignments

The following are typical GCSE coursework and examination assignments.

Coursework

1   Write a review of any performance of *Henry V* – on stage or screen – that you have seen. Say in what ways it fulfilled, fell short of or surpassed your expectations, and whether it changed your view of the play. Support your comments by detailed reference to the text.

2   Read *Henry IV, Parts 1 and 2*. Show how Prince Henry's character changes when he becomes King. Illustrate the ways in which he is recognizably the same person. Say whether you find the changes convincing.

3   Imagine you are directing a production of *Henry V*. Explain what you would do to bring out important qualities (such as dramatic tension, humour, poetic expression) in any one act of the play. Describe the sets, costumes, lighting and sound effects you would use, and indicate the guidance you would give the actors in interpreting their characters.

Coursework/exam questions

4   Some people think that *Henry V* gets off to a slow start. What do you consider to be the importance to the play as a whole of:
    a the opening scene between the two bishops

    b the Archbishop's speech to Henry about his rights to France

    c the attempted treason and its discovery?

5 In Shakespeare's time, theatres lacked the technical resources of elaborate scenery, lighting, sound effects etc which are available today. How does Shakespeare overcome this problem in *Henry V*? Provide detailed textual evidence to support your answer.

6 The Archbishop says 'The King is full of grace and fair regard'. Pistol calls him 'a heart of gold, A lad of life'. Does Henry deserve the praise and loyalty he receives throughout the play?

7 Many plays about war contain a political message. Did *Henry V* have a message for its Elizabethan audience, and does it have one for us today?

8 Some critics think that Fluellen is one of Shakespeare's most attractive and memorable creations. Others feel that he is an irritating and even offensive national stereotype. What is your opinion?

9 On the night before a battle, soldiers often write letters to their families. Write the letter that might have been written by one of the English camp on the eve of the battle of Agincourt. The letter should contain comments on the campaign so far, the writer's view of the King, and his feelings about the coming battle. Write in modern English.

10 Henry says to Katherine 'At night, when you come to your closet, you'll question this gentlewoman about me'. Write the dialogue that might take place between the French princess and Alice after the betrothal of the princess to Henry. Your dialogue should show the impression made by the English king on the French court, and the feelings of the princess about her future. Write in modern English.

11   The closing lines of the play remind us that the
     successors to Henry V 'lost France and made his
     England bleed'. Do you find this pessimistic ending
     surprising, or has the play prepared us for it?

12   In what ways can a modern audience enjoy the comic
     scenes in *Henry V*?

13   Would you agree that the purpose of the Chorus in
     Henry V is not only to help us to visualise events, but
     also to tell us how we should react to them? Support
     your answer by close reference to the text.

14   What do the women characters add to the interest of
     Henry V?

15   From your reading of the play, say what qualities you
     think Shakespeare considered to be necessary in a good
     king.

16   'The French nobles in *Henry V* are caricatures rather
     than characters'. Explain and illustrate this statement
     and say whether, in your opinion, Shakespeare's rather
     one-sided version strengthens or weakens the play as a
     whole.

Textual questions

17   Read *Act 3 Scene 1*. Explain what effects Shakespeare
     is aiming for in Henry's famous speech and show how
     he achieves them. Then explain how the following
     scene contrasts with it, and why Shakespeare has
     created this contrast.

18   Read *Act 3 Scene 5*. What new information does this
     scene give about the progress of the war? How does the
     language convey the national pride of the French and
     their contempt for the English? What future events in
     the play are foreshadowed here?

291

19 Henry is a great orator who can speak powerfully and effectively to crowds, small groups or individuals. Show how any two of his speeches achieve their effects.

20 Read *Act 4 Scene 1*. What different moods and thoughts does Henry reveal during this scene? How does the language of the scene reflect these changes of feeling?

One-word-answer quiz

1 Of what material does the Chorus say his theatre is built?

2 What is the theatre's shape?

3 What was the town of King Henry's birth?

4 From which of his ancestors does Henry's claim to France derive?

5 What is the name of the law which stood between him and the French throne?

6 To which king is this law attributed?

7 In what year did this king die?

8 What 'treasure' does the Dauphin send to Henry through the French Ambassadors?

9 In what year of Henry IV's reign was a bill proposed to tax the clergy?

10 How much a year was the Church to pay the king's exchequer?

11 In which battle did the Black Prince defeat the French?

12 According to an old saying, where must the battle for France begin?

13 Who is said to be 'in Arthur's bosom'?

14 What is Mistress Quickly's Christian name?

15 Who married her?

16 What is the name of her tavern?

17 Who cannot kiss her goodbye?

18 Whose servant, at the beginning of the play, is the Boy?

19 How many shillings does Bardolph owe Nym?

20 How many pence does Fluellen give Williams?

21 How much does Fluellen give Pistol to mend his head?

22 How many hundred crowns does Pistol's prisoner offer as ransom?

23 What is this prisoner's surname?

24 What is the surname of the Constable of France?

25 With what is his armour decorated?

26 Who is the most senior in rank of the English traitors?

27 Two English ports are mentioned by the Chorus; one is Dover, what is the other?

28 At which French port does Henry disembark?

29 What does Bardolph steal, and then carry twelve leagues?

30 What does he steal that costs him his life?

31 In the walls of which town do the English army make a breach?

32 Who is in charge of planting explosives there?

33 What is his nationality?

34 How many hundred paces divide the two camps at Agincourt?

35 Who measures them?

36 On which Saint's Day is the battle fought?

37 On which Saint's Day do Welshmen wear leeks?

38 How many Frenchmen are there for every Englishman at Agincourt?

39 How many Frenchmen are killed?

40 How many Englishmen are killed?

41 At what time does the Duke of Bourbon put on his armour?

42 At what time do the other French nobles put on theirs?

43 What colour is the Dauphin's horse?

44 Who leads the English vanguard?

45 Who dies at the side of the Earl of Suffolk?

46 Who gives King Henry a glove?

47 From whose helmet does the King pretend he had taken it?

48 Who teaches Katherine her first words of English?

49 Which French duke brings the English and the French to the conference table?

50 What is the name of the patron saint of France?

What's missing?

Complete the following quotations.

1 Now all the youth of England are on fire,
   And . . .

2 We few, we happy few . . .

3 Kill the poys and . . .

4 I thought upon one pair of English legs
   Did . . .

5 Oh, Kate, nice customs curtsy . . .

6 If ever thou come to me and say, after tomorrow, 'This
   is my glove . . .'

7 Yea, at that very moment. Consideration like an
      angel came
   And . . .

8 'In terram Salicam mulieres ne succedant . . .'

9 Big Mars seems bankrupt in that beggared host,
   And . . .

10 The country cocks do crow, the clocks do toll,
    And . . .

11 For I do know Fluellen valiant,
    And . . .

12 Cheerly to sea; the signs of war advance; . . .

13 Then call we this the field of Agincourt,
    Fought . . .

14 Once more unto the breach, dear friends, once
       more . . .

15 What a wretched and peevish fellow is this King of
England, to . . .

16 The man that once did sell the lion's skin . . .

17 Sauf votre honneur, en verite vous prononcez les
mots . . .

18 We would not die in that man's company . . .

19 What rein can hold licentious wickedness
When . . .

20 . . . mean and gentle all
Behold, as may unworthiness define . . .

21 And what have kings that privates have not too . . .

22 Oh for a muse of fire, that . . .

23 I Richard's body have interred new,
And . . .

24 Good Bardolph, put thy nose between his sheets,
and . . .

25 I am afeared there are few die well that die in a battle,
for . . .

26 I will cap that proverb with . . .

27 He threw his wounded arm, and kissed his lips,
And . . .

28 Ha, art thou bedlam? Dost thou thirst, base
Trojan . . .

29 He is indeed a horse, and . .

30 I did never know so full a voice issue . . .

31 And let not Bardolph's vital thread be cut
With . . .

32 Old men forget; yet all shall be forgot . . .

33 If you would take the pains but to examine the wars of
Pompey the Great, you shall find . . .

34 Follow your spirit, and upon this charge
Cry . . .

35 'If that you will France win . . .'